HOW TO MANAGE MANAGERS

A WORKBOOK
FOR MIDDLE
MANAGERS

■ ▰ *HOW TO MANAGE MANAGERS*

A WORKBOOK FOR MIDDLE MANAGERS

Härje Franzén
and
Maurice Hardaker

McGRAW-HILL BOOK COMPANY

London · New York · St Louis · San Francisco · Auckland
Bogotá · Caracas · Lisbon · Madrid · Mexico
Milan · Montreal · New Delhi · Panama · Paris · San Juan
São Paulo · Singapore · Sydney · Tokyo · Toronto

Published by

McGRAW-HILL Book Company Europe

Shoppenhangers Road, Maidenhead, Berkshire SL6 2QL, England

Telephone 0628 23432

Fax 0628 770224

British Library Cataloguing in Publication Data

Franzen, Harje

   How to Manage Managers: Workbook for

   Middle Managers

   I. Title   II. Hardaker, Maurice

   658.43

   ISBN 0-07-707944-2

Library of Congress Cataloging-in-Publication Data

This data is available from the Library of Congress,

Washington DC, USA

1234 CL 9654

Typeset by BookEns Ltd, Baldock, Herts.

and printed and bound in Great Britain by Clays Ltd, St Ives plc

Contents

CONTENTS

Preface

This book is for middle managers, a critically important but often maligned group of people whose role is changing rapidly. Yet, there is very little practical help for middle managers. The assumption tends to be that, if you have learned the skills of a first-line manager and you are promoted, then it is just more of the same thing. It isn't. The job is different, and it is different to the job of a top manager, someone who reports directly to the Chief Executive Officer (CEO).

Whereas there is much advice, guidance, literature, training programmes and so on for the extreme levels of management—for first-line managers and for top managers—there is very little that we could find for those in between, the middle managers. And the job *is* different. This book focuses on the differences, on those aspects of a middle manager's job that are specific to this role.

So, it is not aimed at first-line managers at all, though they will benefit from reading it to understand the differences, which are considerable, between their current job and that of their boss. It will also help them to prepare for the day when, who knows, they may be promoted to a middle management job.

It is not aimed directly at top managers, but they also should benefit greatly from reading it, if only to understand the way the nature of the middle manager's job has changed since they were doing it. Besides, you will see that we define a middle manager as a manager of managers. Top managers are *also* managers of managers. While recognizing that the *nature* of a top manager's job is different, the 'manager of managers' aspect still applies. There is much here that is relevant to top managers.

The purpose of this book is to help you to become a better middle manager, but you cannot become a better middle manager simply by reading it, or any other book. Your skills have to be developed in practice, working with real people (*your* people) in real situations. We provide a *structure* for you to do the work of self-improvement, but *you* have to do the work.

The book is intentionally general in approach. It is not focused on any particular industry. It is equally appropriate for middle managers in non-commercial enterprises, such as government, the civil service, police, charities, educational establishments and so on. For this reason, we shall use the word 'enterprise' to describe the place where you work, rather than 'company' or 'firm'. Your enterprise could be a hospital, a business unit, the French subsidiary of a German multinational, a research laboratory, a government department, corporate headquarters, a university.

This book makes no assumptions regarding gender, race, religion, politics and so on— they are beyond our scope. Numerous specialized works exist for consultation on these matters.

Culturally, it is set in what may loosely be termed a 'Western' culture—that is, the setting in which we, the authors, have earned our livings and gained our experience. But it is an international, even global Western culture, and we have tried to reflect this in the book. We hope it works. After all, one of us is a Swede, the other, an Englishman living in France, and our publisher is the European subsidiary of a US-based global publishing house!

How to use this book

This is a workbook, and the person who does the work is you. It is full of practical advice, check-lists and so on, and tasks for you to do. We have arranged it in a logical sequence, taking an assumed newly appointed middle manager through a carefully planned series of ideas, situations and concepts for you to practise in your real world. While each topic stands alone, there is a common connecting thread running through them.

Nevertheless, we do not recommend starting at the beginning and working methodically through the book. We are assuming that you are an experienced manager already. You may even be an experienced *middle* manager, wanting to improve. Instead, we suggest you skim read quickly through the text. This way, you will quickly see the topics we cover and the connections between them, their mutual dependencies. *Then* you can go back to the beginning and attack the tasks and check-lists. It is worth going through all of them, even if you are already an experienced middle manager. You will learn new things about your people and yourself, and you will better prepare yourself for your *next* job.

A word on the check-lists. Like the book, they are general, and often quite copious as a result. Their purpose is to provide a starting point for your own, personal, industry, enterprise, situation and time-specific check-lists. Your personal check-lists will probably be much shorter, and they will almost certainly (we hope) include items that you have added to our lists. *Then* they will be specific to *you* and, as such, much more relevant, practical and valuable.

PART 1

THE CHANGING MIDDLE MANAGEMENT JOB

What is a middle manager?

Maybe you do not think of yourself as a middle manager; perhaps your job title is Manager of Logistics or Chief Officer for Sanitation or Head of the Legal Department or Chief Inspector of Police or Head of Surgery or Manager of Northern Regional Sales Office. So, let us start with a definition of exactly what we mean by the title 'Middle Manager' as used throughout this book.

> **Other managers report to you. They have personnel or managers reporting to them. And you are not (yet) a top manager; someone who reports directly to your Chief Executive.**

This means that any enterprise with three or more management layers between the Chief Executive and any employee has middle managers.

So, your immediate subordinates are *managers*. They may be managers of managers also so, they, too, would be middle managers. There could be seven or eight layers of middle managers where you work, or even more. Whereas the principal aim of this book is to help the recently appointed middle manager, the concepts apply equally well to a middle manager of *other* middle managers, and, as a logical extension of this aim, to top managers.

As we shall see, the number of layers is decreasing almost everywhere. General Motors has streamlined from 28 to around 19, and is still decreasing. Toyota has gone from over 20 to 11 layers.

The definition says nothing about where you came from to the job. You may have worked your way up in the same department or function or division of the same enterprise. Your subordinates may even be your former colleagues. You may have been appointed from a different function or business unit within the same enterprise. Despite working for the same enterprise, your new subordinates may all be total strangers. Alternatively, you may have been appointed from outside the enterprise, so your subordinates, colleagues and bosses will probably all be strangers.

The definition says nothing about the nature of the enterprise. It may be a commercial company or a government department, a charitable organization or whatever.

It says nothing about the enterprise's organization structure. It may be organized by function—finance, marketing, manufacturing, personnel, research and development departments and so forth—or it may be by geography, product group or strategic business unit. It may even be structured around the key cross-functional business processes, though this is still rare. It may be one of the even more rare 'fluid' organizations, with short- or long-lived teams assembled from the skill resources of the enterprise. But don't let anyone kid you that you are working for a 'virtual corporation' or any other such academic abstraction. Look at the name of the enterprise on your payslip. *That* is who you work for, and so do the people who formally report directly to you.

Whatever the structure, style or industry, as long as there are those three or more management layers between the CEO and any employee, there are middle managers.

That wise old management guru Peter Drucker has said that he expects the number of management layers to halve over the next 20 years or so. He expects that there will be only a third the number of managers. Nevertheless, this means that there will continue to be middle managers, despite the flattening of organizations and the 'delayering' that is happening today. However, the middle managers who remain will have to be pretty special.

Welcome to the job! People like you are going to be needed for the foreseeable future. However, the job has changed, and it is still changing. It is getting more difficult, particularly in the apparently more ambiguous world of business process management which many organizations are moving to today. This contrasts with the rigid, functional structures, with nice clean boundaries, which still predominate. These structures are changing too, however.

Changing organizations, shifting populations

To set the scene for our book, and to understand the changing nature of the middle manager's job, now and in the future, we shall take a brief stroll through the recent history of organizations.

Most of us have spent our working lives in highly structured, hierarchical organizations. It was not always like this. The typical nineteenth-century enterprise was more like that shown in Figure P1.1; pretty well all the knowledge and information were concentrated in the thin top layer.

The more currently common 'command and control' structure on the left in Figure P1.2 evolved from the armed services, particularly after the Second World War. It served well in the post-war growth years, when simply to be in business was usually enough to make money. The demand and growth provided lots of opportunities to move up the management ladder, and to add more rungs. Even today, as we have seen with General Motors, some companies have nearly 20 levels between the CEO and the new employee. Lots of middle managers there!

THE NINETEENTH-CENTURY ENTERPRISE

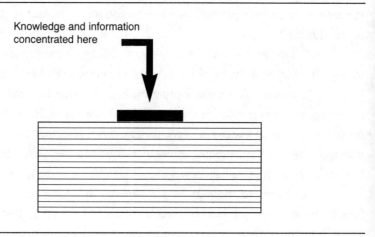

Knowledge and information
concentrated here

Figure P1.1

THE POST-SECOND WORLD WAR ENTERPRISE

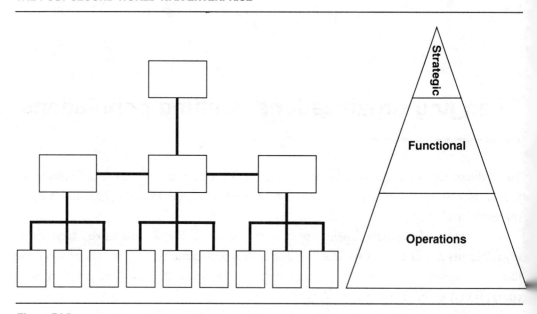

Figure P1.2

The management triangle on the right in Figure P1.2 is another way of representing this structure. The number of people employed at any level decreases as you move up the triangle.

Things started changing in the 1960s and 1970s with the introduction of computers. They automated many of the transaction processing jobs, such as payroll, general ledger,

THE CHANGING ENTERPRISE: THE IMPACT OF TASK AUTOMATION

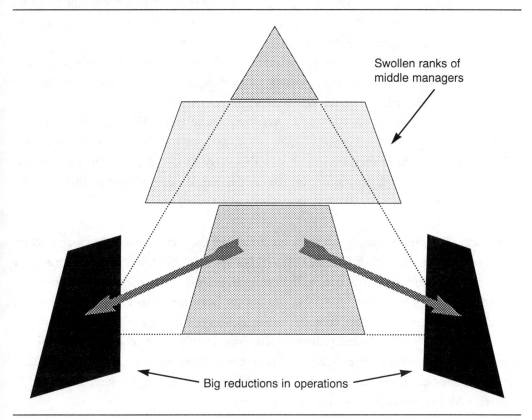

Swollen ranks of
middle managers

Big reductions in operations

Figure P1.3

accounts payable and maintaining stock records. The management triangle changed to
something like that shown in Figure P1.3.

The piece at the top remained about the same size. The number of people on the
average board of directors was more or less constant between 1960 and 1980. It may even have
become slightly larger with the addition of new directors for new functions, such as
'Personnel', 'Finance' (yes, some companies are still creating a finance director for the first
time), 'Information Services' and so forth.

At the bottom, the numbers decreased dramatically, as a result of computer-based
transaction processing.

Note, however, that the bit in the middle grew. This is where we find the middle
managers, and they were able to block and delay things, particularly if any associated changes
were perceived as a threat.

In 1982, Lucas Aerospace embarked on a huge project to computerize the
manufacturing operation. The project leader was the CEO himself. He said he was

betting his business on the success of the project. In effect, he was rebuilding his factories around the software, and *he* ran the weekly project meetings, very vigorously. It was a highly visible, hands-on commitment from the top.

He also organized computer education for himself and his Board members. There was extensive education and training for the people on the shop floor. All the unions were involved and for the new system. Sounds perfect.

A year later, the CEO said, 'We very nearly failed. We ignored the middle managers. We just assumed they would see the benefits to the company, and welcome the change. Instead, they tended to ignore it or reject it'. The situation was saved by a crash programme focused on the middle managers, but it was a close run thing.

This story is far from unique. Much the same thing happened at an Esso refinery around the same time. Another example is Scandinavian Airlines System (SAS). It was named Airline of the Year in 1983 after its CEO personally drove a massive service quality improvement programme. The main agent of change was a very large investment in customer service education for all field personnel, but the managers between the Board and the field people were ignored. Many setbacks and problems were subsequently experienced as a result of this. A much more recent study of the service industry in the United States showed that in virtually every large-scale change effort, one of the most stubborn problems was resistance from middle managers. Middle managers began to get a bad press.

The job starts to change

In many companies middle managers' jobs changed. Formerly, they translated the strategic decisions from the top into revenue-generating actions. Later, as their numbers and layers grew, they became mere collectors and filters of information. They were able to block or massage information on the way up.

Sadly, many top managers still suffer from 'the Persian Messenger Syndrome', where the king kills whoever brings the bad news. Many middle managers understood this syndrome. After all, few companies promote the people who carry *bad* news up the organization chart.

The dramatic fall of IBM may be partly explained by this. After 1992 losses of $6.9 billion on sales of $64.5 billion, IBM's shares sank to an 18-year low of less than $42 and the CEO, John Akers, was replaced by Louis V. Gerstner. It is conceivable that John Akers did not really know just how bad things were in IBM until he read about it in *The Wall Street Journal*. There were too many insulating layers promoting their own interests. Apparently, he was not alone. *Business Week* (2 August, 1993) quoted a source close to the IBM Board claiming, 'The people on the executive committee all should have resigned. None knew what was going on, and they all should have known'.

We shall return to this theme later. Meanwhile, if your managers bring you nothing but good news, watch out. Things are never *that* good. (This applies particularly to personnel issues. They can normally be kept hidden from you for much longer than poor business performance, and the consequences can be correspondingly more serious.)

Large staff groups began to be created. They started to dominate the operations people, who actually made and sold things, and the operations people were the community closest to the customers. These dominant staff groups began to be spoken of disparagingly as 'the bean counters', and they were expensive!

Things began to change in the late 1970s, initially in the United States, where it is typically easier to 'separate' people (what used to be called firing them) than in Europe.

The role of information technology

For a time, information technology helped to preserve some middle managers in their fortresses. In the 1970s, most enterprises relied on a central data processing department. The computer technologists cracked the whip. Then, mini computers became available. By and large, they were forbidden by the central computer people, of course. Soon, a mini computer came to be defined as, 'Any computer that can be hidden in a middle manager's budget' (you could very quickly count up 15 different office machines that were individually programmable and for which the word 'computer' never featured on the invoice). It was a way in which to get around the tyranny of the computer people and their two-and-a-half year backlog of work. It was also a way around the central site's high standards of hardware selection, software, security, standards of operating hygiene, data management, programming, documentation and so on.

THE CHANGING ENTERPRISE: THE IMPACT OF DECISION SUPPORT SYSTEMS

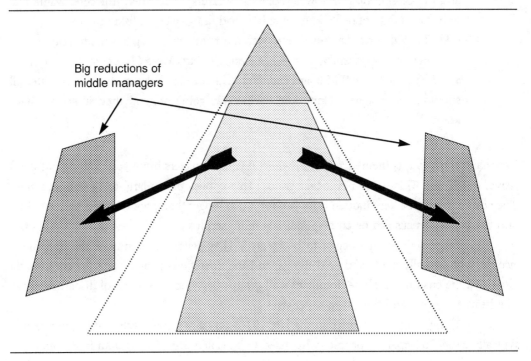

Big reductions of
middle managers

Figure P1.4

Quite soon, to the despair of the mainframe computer people, incompatible islands of automation sprang up all over the place. Each one was sufficiently unique to preserve the boundaries of the mini-empire that it served. But not for long.

Figure P1.4 shows what happened. It was driven by computer departments evolving from being mere processors of data—transaction processing—to being providers of information. PCs began to proliferate in the early 1980s and brought added impetus, and they were so cheap that they could almost be paid for from the stamp tin. In complete contrast to the nineteenth century, information and knowledge were spread throughout the enterprise. Thus, quite quickly, the people who actually took decisions had the necessary information before their eyes—on time, unfiltered, unpolluted—and they had the power to evaluate alternatives at their fingertips. Those who simply made recommendations became redundant.

Some of the information does not even pass before the eyes of real people nowadays. Computers handle it directly.

McKesson, the US pharmaceutical products wholesaler, captured customer loyalty by giving hand-held terminals to pharmacists—McKesson's customers. The pharmacist could see what products were in stock, place the order and print the price labels. In return, McKesson provided guaranteed and fast delivery. Quite soon, thousands of pharmacists were entering purchase orders directly on to McKesson's computer systems. The number of McKesson sales representatives shrank dramatically, and the ones who remained found that their jobs changed. They became much more concerned about customer needs, some of which translated into a broader (profitable) product range in response to a known, quantifiable market requirement.

Then, McKesson went on-line to its over 2000 suppliers, the pharmaceutical manufacturers and so forth. Today, over half of McKesson's own purchase orders are placed computer to computer, automatically. The number of people employed in the Purchasing Department went down from 140 to 13. Fewer sales representatives, fewer buyers, fewer managers.

McKesson has changed itself from being a buyer and seller of products into a dynamically self-balancing money machine located between the highly scattered people with the needs and the people who make the products.

The McKesson situation is highly structured. In the new organizations, information and networking will be all-pervasive. When professionals and managers throughout an organization can communicate with each other this way, horizontal links between peers in different locations—and beyond the enterprise—become established, regardless of any formal organization structure. Yet, such links are important, for people to lend a hand to each other or provide some information, a practical tip. Once, it was thought that information technology would depersonalize the enterprise, but now we see it as binding scattered employees into an integrated whole. Texas Instruments illustrates this on a global scale.

In 1987, Texas Instruments set up a software centre in Bangalore, in India. The people there design the software for custom-made integrated circuit chips for Texas Instruments' customers. They are on-line via satellite communications to Texas Instruments' headquarters in Dallas, and to other locations in the United Kingdom, France, Tokyo and Singapore, for example. The designers in Bangalore can design something, send it to other Texas Instruments locations and get it back, with comments and suggestions, by the end of the same day. Texas Instruments claims a design time reduction of up to 67 per cent. This not only reduces costs for Texas Instruments, it means the customer can introduce the product for which the design was contracted more quickly.

This is a win-win situation for Texas Instruments and for its customers. However, it raises some difficult questions about managing projects and people in this sort of networking environment. Further, the designers are probably on-line to at least some of their customers as well, adding another layer of complexity.

In a growing number of enterprises, these *horizontal* ties between people are replacing the old *vertical* ties as the means of activity and communication, *even where the old vertical structures remain formally in place*. It makes it more difficult to manage people and projects when they are scattered all over the place, particularly when many of the people do not report to the same manager. Yet, the business benefits, in terms of reduced costs and shorter cycle times, make it inevitable. You and your managers are going to have to come to terms with these ambiguities where you do not have the old command authority. You are going to be working permanently with people who work for you, but who are not your employees. Equally, your employees will be working for people who are not their manager.

More beans, fewer bean counters

By April 1983, *Business Week* was able to publish a special report entitled 'The New Era For Management'. One company president was quoted as saying, 'We've been rewarding bookkeepers as if they created wealth ... business has to make more beans rather than count them several times.'

Even in 1983, the article quoted many large US companies that had already got rid of thousands of middle managers. Do you feel secure? It is happening in Europe now, though many middle managers are still unaware of the threat. A survey by the British Institute of Management (BIM) carried out in 1992 addressed 1000 middle managers. Of these, 75 per cent were confident of remaining managers throughout their careers, and 75 per cent were expecting promotion in the near future. Not a single one saw demotion as a possibility. Total Quality Management (TQM) was seen as the biggest driving force for change. Even here, two-thirds of the middle managers expected no change for them.

The BIM survey in 1993 again showed that few managers felt that their own jobs were at risk. Fewer than half of them were worried about future promotion opportunities or their own future job security. Only a handful confessed to a fear of downgrading or worse, or recognized that it might be a good idea to explore the possibility of self-employment or early retirement. A *small* change since 1992, but not a substantial one.

In contrast, top managements' view was that middle managers would be bearing a greater burden, and that their work would be done differently. There would be more emphasis on team working. Pay would be tied to performance. Middle managers would have to evolve to become generalists rather than specialists, which was exactly as predicted by *Business Week* in 1983.

Who is right? Our money is on top managements' view and the historical record. Middle managers are an endangered species, like the giant panda or the three-toed newt. However, unlike the panda, you cannot be covered by a protection order. You have to evolve. Remember, all the dinosaurs are dead. Our aim is to help you through this evolution, even if you are already an experienced middle manager. The rules are changing with the job.

Quality and competitiveness

In one respect, the respondents to the BIM's survey were probably right. TQM must be seen as the biggest driving force for change. By this we do not mean the TQM that gets a tick and a star from some national or international standards organization or whatever; we mean the TQM that is equated with maximizing the total *competitiveness* of the enterprise. Significantly, virtually all the quoted exemplars of TQM have got there by focusing on making their core business processes more competitive rather than by institutionalizing 'Quality'. Consider McKesson and Texas Instruments, for example.

However, we believe that the respondents to BIM's survey were wrong to suppose that TQM would involve no change for them. Indeed, middle managers should be critical agents of change, those middle managers who evolve and survive, that is.

Many of Britain's 500 largest companies complain that middle managers have not supported or understood TQM, according to a survey by the marketing consultants Abram, Hawkes in 1993. Less than 50 per cent of the companies were satisfied with TQM and only 8 per cent were very satisfied. This is not necessarily a case of cause and effect, but our own experience of the cynical rejection of TQM programmes by middle managers adds weight to the argument. In fairness, it must be said that much of the rejection that we saw was caused by a perception that *top* management was really only paying lip-service to the TQM approach, so why bother?

Power flows down, and out

Of course, the 'power' middle managers have has been reduced. It is said that information is power. Compare the nineteenth-century enterprise with today, where information is dispersed throughout the enterprise, and beyond. Inevitably there is 'empowerment' in this situation, whether or not there is a formal enterprise empowerment programme, whatever that means. And empowerment always flows downwards. This can only take away the manager's right to direct, or even fully understand, the work of so-called subordinates. As we said earlier, you have to come to terms with this.

Also, it is flowing out beyond the enterprise. Consider McKesson again. Customers and suppliers (and computers) are doing some of the work now that was formerly done by McKesson people, and the chains are getting longer.

> DuPont makes fibres. It is on-line to Milliken, which makes fabrics. Milliken is on-line to Leslie Fay, which makes garments, which is on-line to Dillards, which sells them in its department stores. This 'extended enterprise' can respond quickly and profitably to changes in the market-place. Information is shared throughout. It *must* be.

McKessen, Texas Instruments, DuPont, Milliken, Leslie Fay and Dillards still have middle managers, of course, though fewer than ten years ago. These middle managers have a very important job to do. Whereas the 'real' work will increasingly be done by cross-functional teams, even in enterprises that retain the familiar (though flattened) organization structure, excellence of the management resource will be even more important than ever. This excellence is your responsibility.

The total quality of management

This *quality of management* is what distinguishes the consistent winners from the losers. This is how important it is. Wonderful technology is not what counts, nor beautiful buildings. The people who sell information technology, for example, will sell it to *anyone*. They do not discriminate. If it was this simple, we would be surrounded by some very successful companies today, instead of a perception by the CEOs that huge amounts of money have been wasted on computer systems.

An associate professor from Belgium, Van Neevent, was working at the Harvard Business School. He received some funding from IBM to study the relationship between money spent on information technology and the economic success of the enterprise. A year later, Van Neevent had data from about 160 enterprises world-wide, of all sizes and representing all industries. To his dismay, he could find no correlation! He was dismayed because he could see how his research budget from IBM would be likely to be stopped abruptly with a result like this.

Then, he had an idea. He studied the 60 worst enterprises and the 60 best, separately, looking at them in terms of economic success. Surprise! For the 60 best, there was a strong positive correlation between information technology budget and success. For the 60 worst enterprises, there was an equally strong correlation, but a *negative* one. In other words, technology was a symptom rather than a cause of success. The distinguishing feature was the quality of management. It was so good in the successful companies that they were able to exploit the technology effectively. For the poorly performing (and poorly managed) companies, the more they spent on computers, the more they accelerated their economic downfall.

Managers and their *people* are the keys to economic success. High-quality management leads to:

- increased productivity
- more competent employees
- key people staying with the enterprise
- fewer problems and less friction within *and* between other groups
- lower turnover of personnel
- mature employees do not mentally retire for their last ten years
- new employees tend to stay (and you recruit the best ones)
- a vital organization, accepting change as a challenge rather than a chore.

These are all important factors today for competitive advantage—even for survival.

Under the old regimes, decision making was largely confined to a middle manager's domain, the defined scope of control that went with the job. Now, you have much less decision-making power. It has been delegated. The scope has been expanded, *but not the control*. Inevitably, there must be an improvement in the quality of management of those to whom so much responsibility has now been delegated. This is one thing. Second, you will have to drive and manage change across a much wider scope of your enterprise than that defined by the boundaries of your domain. *This second requirement needs the first*, a higher quality of management than ever before.

We believe that the key job of middle managers in the future is to improve the total *quality of management* in the enterprise. Other people may be involved from time to time, under the current labels of 'Personnel', or 'Management Development', for example. The Personnel function may lay down policies and programmes, but management quality is a line job. The direct relationship between you and the managers reporting to you means you are ideally positioned to improve the quality of management.

So, as long as there are three or more levels of management, and you are not in either the top or the bottom layer, you have a critically important and challenging job. This book is here to help.

■ *PART 2*

ACCLIMATIZING TO THE NEW ROLE

Welcome to the job

So, now you are in your new job.

After you have removed the pieces of fluff and the old paper-clips from your desk drawers, what next?

It depends. The induction for your new job may have been excellently done, though this is rare. On the other hand, your new boss might have shown you your office, introduced your people, invited you to 'drop in and see me at any time' and then became totally invisible.

We will assume that your induction was less than excellent, so it is largely up to you. Think about the managers *you* will be appointing in the future. How can you be sure *they* become (enthusiastically) productive as quickly as possible? We will come back to this later in Part 5, under 'Induction of new managers'.

Definition of terms

Here are some terms we shall use throughout the book.

A MANAGER
: Someone with personnel responsibility. (We shall use small 'p' personnel to mean people employed by the enterprise. Capital 'P' Personnel will be used to describe the organizational entity with responsibility for personnel issues, sometimes called Human Resources.)

YOUR MANAGER
: The manager who is your boss.

YOUR MANAGERS
: The managers who report to you.

YOUR DEPARTMENT
: The scope of the enterprise over which you have responsibility. Your domain, if you prefer. It may be a traditional organization unit, such as 'Production Control' or 'Accounts Payable' or 'Customs and Excise'; a function, such as 'Marketing', or 'Surgery', or a 'Regional Crime Squad'; or it may be one or more business processes, such as 'Process Customer Orders', 'Distribute Products', for example.

For purposes of providing a coherent structure, we shall continue to assume you have been promoted from somewhere within your current enterprise. Of course, this need not be the case as middle managers are sometimes appointed from outside, but the internal route is more common. However, we shall discuss the 'appointment from outside' situation whenever the differences are important.

You should not be expected to 'hit the ground running', but that probably is the expectation anyway, *so you must become effective in your new job quickly!*

Leaving your old job behind you

Sometimes it is hard to leave your old job behind you. You may have been in the middle of several projects in which you invested a large amount of physical and intellectual energy. It would have been rewarding to see them to fruition. Then there may be the wrench of separating from an excellent winning team that you helped to create. (Maybe that is one reason for your promotion?) You may feel they depend on you personally to carry it forward.

However, the manager who replaced you is expected to 'hit the ground running', too, and you (uniquely) know the ground. You have a key role to play, but the separation from your previous job must be as quick and as surgically clean as possible. This applies particularly if you have been appointed from outside. You should not assume the luxury of going back to your former employer after you have started with the new.

Another thing. You are an experienced manager now. You are strong enough to stand on your own feet. Your replacement may be totally new to the job of manager (we address this issue of entirely new managers in detail in Part 5, under 'New manager's development').

We shall be asking you to do some work quite frequently throughout this book. After all, it is supposed to be a *work*book. The idea is that you can add your experience and perspective to what we have collected in these pages. As an experienced manager, you *must* have something of value to add. Please take your time and think carefully about the questions we ask or the issues we raise, then write down your views.

The model 'solutions' we offer from time to time are just that; models. They can neither be perfect nor complete. Also, the 18 check-lists that are provided are not meant to be accepted wholesale. We suggest you ruthlessly prune them to include only what will be of value to you, *and use them as a starting point to make your own, personal lists*, adding those missing items you believe should be included. This is why it is important to devote a bit of time to the questions, and capture your views by writing them down. Your check-lists will evolve and grow over time. They will be of benefit to you by giving a structure for your thinking in a variety of situations.

A former director of corporate planning at American Telephone and Telegraph (AT and T), Henry Boetinnger, once said, on the subject of recruiting people, 'I look for a quality of mind which can take a vague anxiety, and structure it'. If you can structure your vague anxieties, you can describe them, you can measure them, you can *manage* them.

We expect you to have vague anxieties (at least) from time to time as a middle manager. Your 'personalized' check-lists should help you to structure your anxieties, then manage your way through them.

For the moment, think about the possible pitfalls facing you and your replacement. Let your mind wander over the issues for a few minutes. Then, because this is a workbook, please pick up a pen or pencil and write on it! This is the sort of thing we shall be asking you to do a number of times during the course of this book. Each time, you will know that you have some work to do when the following sign appears.

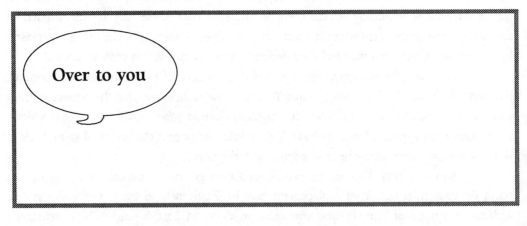

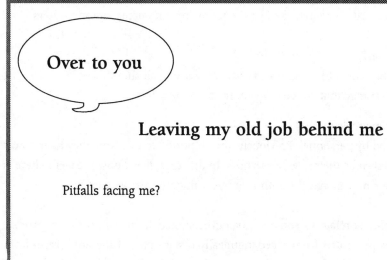

Leaving my old job behind me

Pitfalls facing me?

Pitfalls facing my replacement?

You may have written something like the following comments, among others.

Pitfalls facing me?
Giving priority to my old team. It's easier than learning all about the new teams that report to me. It may initially be a lot more interesting, too.

Pitfalls facing my replacement?
Being bypassed by personnel. Previously, they reported to me. Now they have a new boss. I might even be their new boss's boss. In that case, they know me well. There is danger in their new manager's authority being undermined very early.

Again, these possible pitfalls relate to someone being promoted from within the enterprise. Suppose you have been promoted from a geographically distant part of the enterprise–from Austria to France, for example–or from outside the enterprise altogether. What pitfalls face you in this situation?

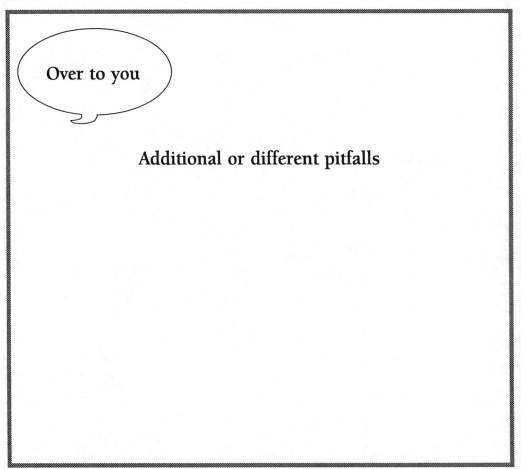

Some possible answers to this question include the following:

> Cultural differences: national cultural differences and differences in style between enterprises, even between functions in the same enterprise, such as between marketing and finance, or legal, for example.

> Carrying your old and proven ways of doing things immediately into the new environment: 'The way we used to approach this in ...'

> Suspicion or resentment from new colleagues and subordinates.

The section in Part 5, 'Induction of new managers', is written with the aim of helping you to become rather better at managing these processes when a new subordinate manager is appointed, reporting to you. It is worth reading from your perspective and applying it to yourself, regardless of where you have come from to the job.

Getting into the new job

Clearly, you have to manage the separation from your old job well, but let us now move on to your rather challenging new job, *after* the separation.

First, you need to be in control of your new job, which involves a very fast rise up the learning curve. Then, when you are in effective charge of your business—not fighting fires and facing crises—you can begin to think more strategically.

The following check-lists will help you to address the key issues, but travelling up the learning curve will require work from you. So,

- work through the check-lists carefully
- highlight any points that strike you as being particularly important for your current situation
- then, write down the actions that you believe you must do to pursue them
- then you can prioritize.

CHECK-LIST 1   Questions to your manager

Many of these are good questions to ask *before* you take a job. Bear them in mind when your next promotion opportunity comes along!

1 Questions specific to our relationship—you as my boss

What are *your* objectives, the objectives of your part of the enterprise?

How do they relate to the objectives of the enterprise as a whole?

How should I contribute to them?

How will I be kept informed about important decisions, projects and other top management activities?

What regular working methods do you want us to have? Routine monthly meetings? Reports? Management committees?

How do you want us to work with performance planning and evaluation?

What routines do you want for individual development planning?

How do we nominate management or promotion candidates?

Am I your permanent deputy in any groups or meetings?

2 Questions about my department

Where are the boundaries with other departments? What is the business scope of my job?

What resources, like machinery and other equipment, belong to my department? What plans are there for renewals?

How do you see the workload of my department in the long term? Stable? Increasing? Decreasing?

How are decisions made about resource levels, objectives, budgets?

Are there any special rules, for example, concerning safety, environmental issues and so on?

What are the overall objectives of my department?

Are the documented business and personnel objectives valid?

Which of my managers will be moving on within three months?

3 Questions about my job

Are there any urgent problems in my new area of responsibility?

What other issues have the highest priority today?

Is there a job description of my position? Is it still valid?

How will I be measured?

Who are my key customers—internal and external? Who depends on the outputs of my department?

What do you believe are their expectations?

How will *they* measure me?

Who are my key suppliers—internal and external?

Who do I need to know to do my job well?

What are my financial responsibilities? What is my authority for signing bills? What has to be signed by you?

What new knowledge do I need?

How can I best acquire this knowledge?

(Please do add your own questions to these and future lists.)

Do not expect your manager to have ready answers to all your questions, and be prepared to present your own proposals and ideas as a basis for discussion.

CHECK-LIST 2 Questions to your predecessor

It is not always practicable to get answers to these questions. Your predecessor may have been fired, retired, promoted to a distant part of the world or transferred to a subsidiary, for example. Your predecessor may even be dead. Let's hope it was not through overwork!

In the case of an orderly transition (such as we hope you are arranging for *your* successor), you can learn a lot by having a well-prepared, formal meeting with your predecessor.

Be very careful not to inherit your predecessor's opinions, however, regarding senior management, colleagues, other people, problems and so forth. You have to take over the job, not the preconceived ideas. Try to form your own opinions, though recognize that this may take some time.

You might start by asking the question, 'Why are you leaving this job?'

Then, look at 'Questions about my department' and 'Questions about my job' in Check-list 1.

Additional questions to your predecessor might include the following.

What information systems am I dependent on? How good are they?

How does the whole thing work in real life? Any unclear areas?

Who are the key people around me—internal and external?

What trade journals or books do you recommend?

Have any of my managers had their current jobs for more than three years?

What are their development plans?

Which of my managers will be moving on within three months?

What changes would you make in the organization, had you remained?

Do you plan to have a final meeting with your managers?

Are there any promises or agreements between you and any of my people that I should know of?

Have you any ideas about individual development plans, job rotation, promotion, and so on, that are not documented?

What would be your priorities, if you were in my situation?

CHECK-LIST 3 Questions to your managers

You should arrange a meeting with each of your managers, individually. Start with an open discussion of each manager's view of current activities, new ideas, priorities, the future, personnel development. Send a suggested list of such topics, but stress that the agenda will be open—anything can be discussed.

Allow plenty of time for this part of the meeting, but tell your managers how long it will be. You don't want them to ramble on for ever. Then, get down to your questions.

1 Questions about the manager's current work

Are there any urgent problems in your area of responsibility?

Which issues have the highest priority today?

What is the status of each of your projects?

Who are your key customers—internal and external?

What are their expectations? What is their current level of satisfaction?

Who are your key suppliers—internal and external?

How well are they meeting your requirements?

How do you see the workload of your group in the longer term?

Have you got a job description? Is it relevant and current?

2 Questions about the manager's personnel

Are there job descriptions for all your staff?

Are you behind schedule with any performance planning and evaluation reviews? Do you *have* such reviews?

Are there any undocumented promises, understandings, agreements or whatever between you and anyone in your group?

Have you any ideas about promotions, rotations, people leaving, recruitment and so on that are not documented?

What is the motivation climate in your group? Are there any obviously dissatisfied members?

Have your people got the right skills to do the job well?

Have they got the right technology?

What is their workload? Are there vacancies in your group?

Who are your key people? Who is your deputy?

When can I meet your group?

3 Questions about the manager's department

What resources are you responsible for, such as machinery and equipment? How good are they? Are there plans for renewals?

What information systems do you depend on? How good are they? What is currently under development?

What other departments do you depend on? How good is the level of cooperation? Is it formally defined?

Are there any special rules or policies applicable to your group, for example regarding safety, security, environmental issues?

4 Questions about my department

What do you think about the current organization of my department?

What is your view on the level of cooperation in my department?

What changes in working methods would you recommend?

You could be excused for believing that this will take an inordinate amount of time, and you would be right–particularly if you add some company-, industry- or job-specific questions of your own.

So, compromise on thoroughness, at least initially. The idea is to meet as many of the key people as soon as possible, with a structured approach to get you quickly up that learning curve. Consider sending a short extract from the check-lists before each meeting. It should help the managers in their preparation and this will help *you*. However, do not send *all* the questions in advance. For some of them, you may prefer to have an answer that has not been premeditated.

The check-lists will help to underline the new roles and relations. After all, your managers may once have been your colleagues. Now you are their boss. Even if they are complete strangers, the check-lists will set the new scene more or less automatically.

Remember, the value to you is not only in the answers to the specific questions, but also in any ensuing discussion. Urgent issues will emerge spontaneously. Don't just listen to the words; listen to how they are said.

Issues arising in a start-up situation

Up to now, we have assumed that you have moved into an established organization that is in full operation. Plans and projects are in place; people and technology, too.

Suppose, though, you are a middle manager appointed to do something new. There is *no* predecessor to talk to, *no* plans to understand, *no* history, *no* problems (no operational ones, at least). You still have to succeed.

What are the major differences between this and the situation we discussed earlier? What is easier? What is more difficult? Reflect on it for a few minutes, then write down your conclusions.

Over to you

Differences: taking on the totally new versus an existing entity

Things that might make it easier.

Things that might make it more difficult.

Which questions can be salvaged from the earlier check-lists?

What new questions are there? Who should you ask?

One clear difference is that you can probably select your own staff, and the managers reporting to you (or at least you should have a large say in the matter). You are probably the first one on board.

It then becomes easier *only* if you have a clear understanding of your mission—the results you have to achieve, and when—and a clear idea of your boundaries and the 'rules of the game', constraints, how you will be measured and so forth. You should have gained a clear understanding of these before you took the job, of course. Look again at Check-list 1, 'Questions to your manager'.

With the knowledge of *what* you must achieve and *what* is your responsibility, *how* you do it is your own business, within the rules of the game.

Now you can start recruiting your managers. You need to generate a whole new list of questions to ensure you get what you want. Are the candidates qualified for, interested in, even inspired by the challenge? What ideas have *they* got to reach the goals? Then you can go back to your manager proposing *how*—strategy, organization, personnel, technology and so on.

This totally new creation is an extreme case. More often, you may have to merge existing organizations into something different. This is hard; people and prejudices already exist. There may be differences in style to reconcile, like mixing manufacturing and development people together to achieve an earlier manufacturing involvement in the product-development process. Old conflicts may have to be resolved and old skeletons relentlessly flushed out of cupboards.

This is typically the situation when an enterprise moves from a functional to a business process focus. Further, it becomes a lot harder when the processes are subject to large changes, as a result of what is being called 'process re-engineering'. It may be splendid for the top management to make these far-reaching, strategic decisions, and vital to the success of the enterprise. Guess who has to make it happen on the ground? Yes. You and your fellow middle managers! Inevitably, the processes are cross-functional and the tensions must be resolved, fast.

The pay-off can be very big, in terms of reduced costs and faster cycle times, for example. Consider again the example of McKesson, the pharmaceutical products wholesaler. You have a key role in getting those big pay-offs in your enterprise.

Another example. The IBM ThinkPad PC resulted from a merger of mutually antagonistic but individually smart departments. Each took a departmental view. This was the way it had always been, and the reward system reflected this view. Marketing thought they would sell only 6000, world-wide, and they did not believe Development could do it, anyway. Development *knew* they could do it, but they had no confidence that Marketing could sell the thing, and they were convinced that Manufacturing would not be able to build it.

By focusing on the brand, rather than on individual departmental excellence, the boundary wars were extinguished. The ThinkPad 700C came out in three months. The market-place liked the product, particularly the screen and the keyboard, and the price-performance was competitive.

Not 6000, but 100 000 ThinkPads were sold in the first 53 days.

Top management made the strategic decision to have a brand focus, but the key people in resolving the conflicts are the middle managers. They have to give the visible lead in cooperating across the old organizational boundaries and make sure that *their* managers follow them.

The Dutch electronics giant Philips Electronics has suffered from chronic internal boundary wars for many years. Research and product development were not coordinated. Marvellous new technologies were going unexploited. New projects were sometimes killed because lower-level managers (middle managers) took a departmental view. They worried about tight budgets or were concerned about protecting existing product lines. Sounds familiar? A new business in automated lighting controls was frozen for two years because of conflicts between the Lighting and the Semiconductor business units. A new committee of divisional executives was formed in 1993 to screen ideas. They brought together the heads of the Lighting and Semiconductor units—middle managers, by our definition. The Lighting unit answered the Semiconductor unit's concerns that the new products might not succeed, and the stalemate was broken. So simple, yet Philips' past is strewn with unexploited opportunities like this.

Management quality is not just a matter of doing the job well by today's accepted rules and ways of doing things—sometimes called paradigms. It also means being equipped to handle the changes necessary to move to *tomorrow's* paradigms; indeed, anticipating and redefining them.

There is an awful lot of talk about 'paradigm shifts' today. This really means challenging the status quo. It means thinking the unthinkable, and we are advocating it. A major paradigm shift at IBM and at Philips Electronics was simply the breaking down of some ancient organizational and cultural boundaries, getting some colleagues to talk to each other. However, even such simple shifts have massive impacts on managers, and on middle managers in particular.

Your task of maximizing the total quality of management to enable these paradigm shifts to be identified or embraced enthusiastically is addressed in Part 3, 'Total Quality and the quality of management'.

Some major pitfalls

First, we shall summarize the major pitfalls facing you as you acclimatize yourself to your new role and advise you on how to avoid them.

1 Don't get involved in details

You must stop behaving like a first-line manager. Work through your managers. Remember the things that are uniquely theirs (planning for their group, problem solving, personnel issues and so on) and keep out of the way. Of course, there will be times when you can and must make a direct contribution. You have wider experience and a broader perspective now. If you manage your managers well, you can wait to be asked.

2 Don't bypass your managers

Your 'symbolic value' is higher as a result of being a middle manager. The decisions you make, the information and the rewards you give are all more valuable as a result of your position. Much as you may like to continue to be 'one of the gang', be careful. You may not only dilute your symbolic value, you will undermine the authority of your managers. Of course, you should be able to have informal discussions about work with anyone and everyone. The point is to avoid interfering in areas that are the province of your managers; all formal matters where someone's immediate manager should be concerned. (Note that there are some enterprises where 'symbolic value' means little or nothing, but you will already know this if you work in one!)

3 Don't give priority to your old group

We touched on this previously. Your successor *will* need more contact with you, at first, than your other managers. Then read pitfall 1 again, and get out of the way.

4 Don't impose your management style on others

You may not recognize it, but you already have a management style. It may have been a significant factor in your promotion. Recognize that your managers have their own styles. Try to understand their strengths, then you can help them to exploit their strengths—to the good of all—rather than impose your own style. You will fail, anyway. Instead, remember your responsibilities to being a role model in order to influence behaviour.

■ *PART 3*

TOTAL QUALITY AND THE QUALITY OF MANAGEMENT

Management—a critical resource

As noted earlier, the quality of management is what distinguishes enterprises that consistently perform well from the rest. By any definition, management must be regarded as a critical resource of the enterprise. Of course, there are other critical resources, and they differ between enterprises. The critical resources of a hospital are different to those of a detergent manufacturer. However, differences in the common resource, *management*, can make the competitive difference between two similar detergent manufacturers. A useful definition of a critical resource is as follows.

> It costs a lot of money to obtain it (examples are land, buildings, plant and equipment) and/or, if not properly cared for, it will cause the enterprise to suffer (examples are skills, products, customers).

Management fits this definition of a critical resource. It satisfies both criteria. One of your key responsibilities as a middle manager is to increase and sustain the quality of this critical resource, *including* the quality of your own management skills.

Study the definition of a critical resource carefully, then write down some of the critical resources of the enterprise where you work today.

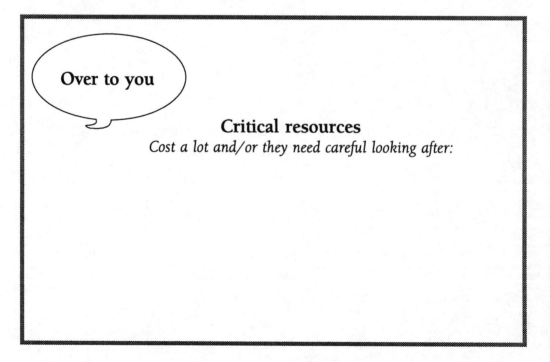

Over to you

Critical resources
Cost a lot and/or they need careful looking after:

We shall use the following list of critical resources to develop our theme.

- brands
- customers
- designs
- information
- inventories
- land and buildings
- management
- materials
- money

- patents
- personnel
- plant and equipment
- political pull
- products
- shareholders
- strategic alliances
- suppliers
- systems

This partial list of resources is arranged alphabetically, but there are differences between them. We can also arrange them this way.

Owned resources

- brands
- designs
- information
- inventories
- land and buildings
- materials
- money
- patents
- plant and equipment
- products
- systems

Resources available to others

- customers
- management
- personnel
- political pull
- shareholders
- strategic alliances
- suppliers

The owned resources in the left-hand column can be locked up at night and you can reasonably expect them to be there the next day, or after the weekend. However, the point is, they can be sold, on behalf of the enterprise as a whole.

The resources in the right-hand column may be just as critical, but you cannot lock them away. You cannot assume that they will be there tomorrow. They can be negotiated away from you, on an individual basis. They are always available to others, your competitors, for example.

> In March 1993, Volkswagen hired José Ignacio Lopez from General Motors, where he had established a reputation for ruthless cost-cutting as Production Director at the Adam Opel unit in Germany. Others defected with him. There goes a big portion of this manufacturer's management resource, to a competitor.
>
> Opel then charged Mr Lopez and his people with taking confidential documents to Volkswagen. Volkswagen counter-charged that General Motors had planted documents at Volkswagen to undermine German industry. In the end, Germany's Economics Minister was talking to both firms to try to stop a row that was doing no good to Germany's reputation.

This kind of corporate conflict might make for good television, but the point is, if Lopez, or anyone else, wants to leave, then they are free to do so. So, too, are your customers and key suppliers.

Of course, your competitor's similar 'non-owned' resources are available to you. The trick is to maximize the quality of the best of *your* right-hand list while negotiating the best away from your competitors, such as their customers, for example.

We can separate out three particular resources from the right-hand list of non-owned resources:

- management
- personnel
- skills.

These three are more 'internal' than customers, suppliers, shareholders and so forth. They are the super-critical resources, if you like, because it is *their* quality that determines how well the *inanimate* resources in the left-hand column can be exploited to acquire and retain the best

- customers
- market share
- political pull

- strategic alliances
- shareholders and so forth.

Also, because high-quality management is needed in order to have the best quality personnel and skills, yours is a critically important job.

Resources and attributes

Some of the following often appear in lists of critical resources:

- competitiveness
- customer satisfaction
- image/reputation
- quality
- credit rating
- employee satisfaction
- market share
- share price.

These are not resources. Rather, they are attributes of the enterprise, or characteristics or properties if you prefer. They are measures of the strength, fitness or power of the enterprise, *and they are determined by people who are outside of the control of your enterprise.*

Notice that it is appropriate to appoint senior people to have responsibility for the critical *resources*. So, we see directors of finance, external affairs, personnel, product development, sales and so forth. But has anyone ever heard of a director of share price or employee satisfaction or credit rating or competitiveness? These *attributes*, these indications of fitness, are the consequences of management's attention (or the lack of it) to the critical resources, and to the business processes to which they are applied.

The job title director of quality is really just as inappropriate as having a director of share price. Total Quality (like share price) is decided outside of the enterprise, *relative to its competitors.* (A director of quality programmes would make sense though, if the title is describing something internal—the enterprise-specific education and training in Total Quality, for example.) Of course, like share price or credit rating or reputation, you try to increase Total

Quality. *You* do not decide what it is, however, your *customers* do. Like all the other attributes, it is not appropriate that it be 'owned' by one person. Like the other attributes, it is everyone's responsibility. As a manager of managers, *their* quality is particularly *your* responsibility.

The life cycle of resources

If a resource is sufficiently critical to appear on your list, it deserves careful management.

It makes it easier to identify the key *processes* of managing a resource if we flow it through its life cycle in the enterprise, as follows:

- *planning processes*   what we will need
- *acquisition processes*   how we get what we will need
- *stewardship processes*   how we look after what we have got
- *disposal processes*   how we release what we have got.

Clearly, there are different processes, or activities, involved in the four phases of the resource's life cycle. If these processes are not understood or are badly performed, under-resourced or missing, the consequences appear sooner or later in the *attributes*—customer satisfaction, share price, Total Quality and so forth.

We are going to ask you to try flowing one resource through its life cycle, writing down the different processes or activities that *should* exist to enable the resource to be effectively planned for, acquired, looked after and disposed of.

Important
When describing a process or an activity in this way, it is useful to use a verb + noun format. Examples are 'develop new products', 'monitor personnel satisfaction', 'define future skill needs', 'bill customers', 'advertise products'. Notice that there are no qualifying adjectives in these process descriptions. 'Develop **superb** new products' is not a process; it is a target, a hope, a dream, perhaps, but not a process.

Hint

When you write down a process, read it. If what you read describes the **result** you want, it is not a process (like 'develop **superb** new products'). For the same reason, the verb 'manage' is not allowed.

It is sometimes quite difficult to come to terms with the discipline of describing business processes this way as there is always the temptation to write targets (like 'improve morale'), but the value of your list will be considerable if you avoid doing this. You will have identified activities that are tangible and capable of improvement, rather than targets that are intangible. We shall come to targets, of course, in Part 4. They will be the targets for process improvement.

Writing down the life cycle for the resource 'products' in this way might produce a result like that below. We have added some notes for the first few to show why these processes might be important for products as a resource.

■ *Planning processes*
Monitor customer complaints.
(What is wrong with current products?)
Monitor competition.
(What have they got? What is good? What are they planning?)
Identify target markets/customers.
(Segments/industries/countries?)
Monitor technology opportunities.
(What can we use? What can we include in new products?)
Define interfaces with existing products.
(If it is an add-on to existing products.)
And so forth.

■ *Acquisition processes*
Negotiate raw material/component supplies.
Develop new products.
Negotiate product production.
Negotiate product procurement.
Make product.
Procure product.
Design product packaging.
And so forth.

■ *Stewardship processes*
Register product patents.

Commercialize products.
Monitor product quality.
Negotiate/release product changes.
Service/maintain installed products.
Monitor customer complaints.
Monitor competition
Review product range.
And so forth.

■ *Disposal processes*
Advertise products.
Demonstrate products.
Offer products for sale.
Process customer orders.
Distribute products.
Install products.
Withdraw products.
And so forth.

This is not meant to be a complete list. Nor is it specific to any particular industry—it could be printing machinery, software, domestic appliances, financial services, whatever. With a little imagination, it could even apply to a national security organization, such as the United Kingdom's MI5. When you do it for *your* products (or any other resource), then it does become industry- and enterprise-specific and, correspondingly, valuable. Then you can start to sequence the processes, for example, and consider which may be sub-processes of others in your particular situation.

Now try it yourself. Choose any of the resources you identified earlier.

Over to you

Your resource ....

■ *Planning processes*

■ *Acquisition processes*

■ *Stewardship processes*

■ *Disposal processes*

The boundaries between the categories of planning, acquisition, stewardship and disposal are arbitrary. In fact, the categories are only there to help to structure your thoughts. Remove them, if you wish. The important thing is to identify *all the key processes needed* for the effective management of each critical resource.

It is to the *processes* that you must allocate your resources, particularly the super-critical ones of management, personnel and skills.

Notice also that the processes will be performed in a number of different *functions*, at least in a 'traditional' hierarchical organization. The successful IBM ThinkPad example quoted earlier illustrates the importance of negotiating across functional boundaries today, or even breaking them down altogether. Top management may well decide to break them down in the name of business transformation or business re-engineering or whatever, but it will be up to *you*, as a middle manager, to make the thing work.

At any point in time, and for any enterprise, some processes on the list are more important than others.

In the late 1960s and early 1970s, the most critical processes for the resource 'personnel' in IBM UK were under the heading 'Acquisition'. The company and its business were expanding rapidly. The nature of its relationship with customers was changing from a technically oriented selling approach to one based on an understanding of the customer's industry and specific business needs.

Large numbers of experienced people were hired (typically in their mid-thirties) who had some years of experience of banking, retail, manufacturing, insurance, oil, government, distribution and so forth. Managements' focus was on the acquisition processes.

By contrast, in the late 1980s and early 1990s, the most critical personnel processes were under the heading of 'Disposal'. That is where management's attention in IBM UK has been focused more recently (and not just in IBM and not just in the UK).

Look again at the resource life cycle that you created earlier.

1 Which are your most critical processes today *for this resource*?

2 How well are they being performed today?

    A = Excellent

    B = Good

    C = Fair

    D = Bad

    E = Process is not currently being performed (but it should be)

Over to you

Your most critical processes   **Process quality today**

There is only one acceptable standard for the quality of your most critical business processes—excellence. Further, you need excellent managers (among other things) to ensure excellent business processes. We discuss these questions of quality and excellence in the next section.

Total Quality/Competitiveness/Effectiveness

There is a strong relationship between Total Quality and competitiveness (for a commercial enterprise) and effectiveness (for a non-commercial enterprise, like a government department). The following definition of Total Quality helps to establish the relationship. It also enables you to define what 'excellence' should mean, when applied to critical business processes. It simply means the description of how the process should perform when it is making the maximum possible contribution to Total Quality, and, as we shall see, this also means the contribution it makes to competitiveness (or effectiveness).

Total Quality equals

Relative product/service price-performance

The quality of what is being offered for sale—value for money.

Multiplied by

Relative customer satisfaction with each 'customer-visible' business process

The quality of the way the customer directly experiences how the business is being run.

(where 'relative' means relative to competition)

This is clearly aimed at commercial enterprises, because of the words 'profit' and 'customer'. We shall modify the definition later, so that it is relevant to non-commercial enterprises, like government.

'Customer-visible' business processes are all those aspects of the business that customers can see or directly experience. Examples are:

- bill customers
- advertise products
- distribute products
- offer products for sale

- demonstrate products
- monitor customer complaints.

Each factor in the definition is on a scale 0 to 1. So, even if your product (or service) is better than anything that can be bought from competitors, in 'value for money' terms, it is not enough. We are talking here about *Total* Quality. This means that if just one customer-visible process is bad enough—and it can be as mundane as not answering the telephone properly—Total Quality becomes zero. One multiplied by zero is zero.

The truth of this is confirmed by a large survey carried out in the United States in the service industry. People were asked which factors influenced them most to change suppliers. Of those questioned, 68 per cent quoted an attitude of indifference by the supplier's personnel. This means bad quality customer-visible processes.

Equally, even if you have the most superb customer-visible processes ('delightful people to deal with'), the product price-performance must *also* compare well with what can be bought from competitors.

The aim is to maximize both factors, simultaneously.

Notice that there are only two basic kinds of business process. There are those that are customer-visible, and there are those the customer does not normally see or directly experience. These 'invisible' processes are equally important. They determine the quality of the first factor in the definition—product price-performance—and they can have a direct impact on the quality of the second factor, the customer-visible processes.

This means that everyone in the enterprise is working in either:

- a customer-visible process or
- an 'invisible' process.

There are no others. So, *everyone* in the enterprise is making a direct contribution (positive or negative) to Total Quality.

Now, we can define what Total Quality is for a non-commercial enterprise.

Total quality equals

Relative service cost-performance   The quality of services available, relative to the best elsewhere.

Multiplied by

Client satisfaction with all   The quality of the way the client directly
client-visible processes   experiences how the enterprise is being run.

(where 'relative' means relative to best-of-breed)

The first factor involves considering how well the services compare with the best supplier of police services, library services, tax collection and so forth in terms of *what is provided and what it costs*. Price is not a consideration because the client normally has no choice. You are stuck with the police force you have got, but you still have to pay. So, relative cost-performance with what the best can do is important.

The second factor involves the 'client-visible' processes, which are analogous to customer-visible processes. A police force can be cost-effective, all right, but contain surly, ill-mannered officers who alienate the general public. This alienation can then have a detrimental effect on other police processes.

Business processes

What determines *Total* Quality is *the quality of each business process*:

- the cost-performance of your invisible processes and
- the cost performance *and* customer satisfaction of your customer-visible processes.

(We shall use the word 'customer' to mean customer or client.)

The quality of each process is determined by the quality of its resources and on how well they are used. This, in turn, implies excellence of the resources of:

- management
- personnel
- skills.

Consider the definition of Total Quality. Change the title to Total *Competitiveness* and we have a definition of *Total Competitiveness*, and the means to measure it. For non-commercial enterprises, it becomes a definition of *Total Effectiveness*. You may not feel exhilarated by the idea of Total Quality (many people have reached the point of exhaustion and disillusionment by official Total Quality Programmes). Everyone should become enthusiastic about the prospect of becoming more competitive, however. Total Competitiveness and Total Quality are the same thing. Take your pick.

As a middle manager, you have to improve the critical resource *management*. We shall use the life cycle approach for this, considering the processes of planning, acquisition, stewardship and disposal of the management resource.

Previously, we asked you to look at the life cycle of processes for just one resource. The next check-list consists of a rather long list of business processes, from a wide range of industries. You will notice that only a few of them are industry-specific, however.

Please study them and identify which processes are necessary for your domain, that part of the enterprise which is yours and your managers'. In particular, look for those processes that will enable you to make the biggest contribution to Total Competitiveness (or Total Effectiveness). As usual, if you need to refer to processes that are not on the list, add your own (please refer to the guidelines on pages 38–9 for defining a business process).

CHECK-LIST 4 A selection of business processes

☐ Advertise products

☐ Announce new products

☐ Bill customers

☐ Communicate company policy and values

☐ Define future skill needs

☐ Define new product requirements

☐ Define/review product range

☐ Develop new products

☐ Develop/review motivation plan

☐ Distribute products

☐ Educate/train suppliers

☐ Educate/train employees

☐ Educate/train suppliers

☐ Forecast product volumes

☐ Identify target markets/customers

☐ Invest liquid funds

☐ Lobby government agencies

☐ Lobby professional agencies

☐ Monitor key account activity

☐ Monitor product quality

☐ Monitor security of sensitive material

☐ Monitor technology opportunities

☐ Monitor total cost

☐ Negotiate operating plan

☐ Negotiate budget

☐ Negotiate selling channels/agencies

☐ Offer products/services for sale

☐ Pay suppliers

☐ Plan facilities' requirements

☐ Plan product demand

☐ Price products

☐ Promote the company

☐ Process customer orders

☐ Purchase parts and raw materials

☐ Recruit personnel

☐ Release engineering changes

☐ Manufacture products	☐ Research the market-place
☐ Market products	☐ Review/modify terms and conditions
☐ Monitor competition	☐ Review/modify product range
☐ Monitor consumer trends	☐ Select and certify suppliers
☐ Monitor customer/prospect's business	☐ Select distribution channels
☐ Monitor customer complaints	☐ Service installed products
☐ Monitor customer satisfaction	☐ Survey personnel satisfaction
☐ Monitor fashion trends	☐ Track finished products
☐ Monitor legislation	☐ Test compliance with environmental
☐ Monitor strategic alliances	requirements

Now, identify which of *your* processes are customer-visible, if any.

If your processes are necessary, their quality should be excellent. What is the quality of each of your processes today?

A = Excellent

B = Good

C = Fair

D = Bad

E = The process does not exist today, but it should.

Over to you

Your most critical processes? Customer-visible? Quality today?

Now you will begin to get an idea about where you and your managers need to focus attention to have the biggest impact on Total Quality/Competitiveness/Effectiveness. Also, because you probably want to make an impact quickly, we shall start with the processes of stewardship. We shall assume that you already have managers. Part 4 describes how you can improve the quality of the resource you have today. We shall return to planning, acquisition and disposal later.

■ *PART 4*

MANAGING THE QUALITY OF MANAGEMENT (I): STEWARDSHIP

Excellent management

The overriding characteristic of excellent managers is that they consistently deliver *results*. There are not many jobs about today where a manager can get paid simply for 'thinking great thoughts'. Excellent managers actively enable their personnel and skill resources to transform the inanimate resources—raw materials, money, information, plant and equipment, designs, brands, systems, whatever—into *results that move the enterprise significantly forwards towards its goals.*

These results do not just happen; they are the consequence of *management* actions and they can be compared with the desired results—the targets. If you can't measure it you can't manage it.

Notice that those 'results that move the enterprise significantly forwards towards its goals' will normally require some innovation, even the taking of risks. Good administrators tend to be gifted at keeping the wheels turning in a given direction, a comparatively simple task compared with management. We are talking here about *management.*

Excellent managers introduce and manage change (and the attendant risks). They can thrive on ambiguity and can prevent their part of the enterprise from disintegrating under pressure. The key thing is, *they deliver results.*

Administrators need to exercise little influence on other people to keep things moving. In contrast, the exercise of influence on others to get results is key to the success of excellent managers.

None of this presupposes that the manager is working in a commercial enterprise. You could just as well be in local government, a National Health Service hospital, a charity organization, the police, the civil service and so forth. There are some different inanimate resources, that is all. The common factor is the *human* resources; personnel and skills. Your *managers* have these resources. As a middle manager, you have your *managers.* (Of course, you may also have non-managerial personnel reporting directly to you, such as your own support staff.)

Stewardship of your management resource means you have to improve to excellence and maintain the quality of what you have. To do this, you will need to:

- know what management resources you have today
- have a clear understanding of what is meant by 'excellence'.

Then you will know the *size* and the *nature* of the gap; the 'delta' that has to be closed, for each of your managers, to attain excellence.

It all sounds simple and almost mechanistic, put like this, but it isn't, of course. Bear in mind that your job involves leadership as well as management, and leadership involves something more than exerting influence on your managers. It also means changing their *values*.

Moreover, leadership is not suddenly bestowed on you with the job title. It evolves over time and has to be earned. To some extent it depends on a recognition of your wisdom, which derives from you being right–good decisions, consistent and predictable results. However, at first, all you have is management experience. Use it well (and soon). Leadership will follow.

Defining the delta of excellence

Let's start by addressing the first point above.

What is the quality of the management resource you have today?

It will take time for you to build up a complete and accurate view of all your managers, but a good start will have been made by using the questions and check-lists of Part 2, 'Acclimatizing to the new role'. This view of your managers will become more detailed and more complete as you use the stewardship tools given here, by the way.

For your stewardship role, you should be considering only those managers who will be there long enough for you to exercise influence–and leadership. For those managers you know will be gone within, say, three months (as a result of retirement, promotion, job moves to another part of the enterprise, reversion to a non-managerial role and so on), you should be considering the disposal processes. This way you should be able to manage an elegant departure for them. Again, you should have identified who will be moving on as a result of using the earlier questions and check-lists.

The second point above looks ahead.

What is meant by 'excellence' of your management resources?

The answer is simple; excellent managers deliver excellent results. It is also your job to define what *they* are–the needed results; your interpretation of what must be the accomplishments within your domain 'that move the enterprise significantly forwards towards its goals'.

We do not discuss *how* to define the needed results in this book. They will vary enormously, depending on your industry, whether it is commercial or non-commercial, on its history, plans and strategies, the environment, politics, the competitive situation and technology, for example. For techniques that can be used to define the needed results for any enterprise, see, for instance, *Total Competitiveness* by Maurice Hardaker (McGraw-Hill, 1994).

To provide a general framework, let us assume that the needed results are to make the maximum possible impact on Total Quality/Total Competitiveness/Total Effectiveness. This very general view could be applied to most situations.

So, the results should have a positive impact either on product/service price-performance (which means good *cost*-performance) or on customer satisfaction with a customer-visible business process, or both. Also, because everyone in the enterprise is working in processes that are either customer-visible or are invisible to customers (there are no others), the principles here apply to *everyone in the enterprise.*

Influences on results

There are five major influences on the results produced by any working group of people (the approach that follows is drawn from *Managing Organisational Behaviour* by C. F. Gibson, Irwin, 1980). If you were to invite someone to visit you in, say, two years' time and they wanted to measure the success of any of your groups, or your entire domain, they would want to see good measurements of improvement in the following factors:

- efficiency
- effectiveness
- employee satisfaction
- the ability to secure scarce or vital resources
- the ability to manage change.

Let us look at each of these in more detail.

Efficiency
How well is the money spent, the time used, and so on? In a process sense, this is asking, how well are the inputs to the process converted to the outputs? You can compare your performance with that of your competitors; better yet, with 'best-of-breed'—whoever does

billing or new product development or brain surgery, for example, better than anyone else in the world.

> What does it cost to process the data to produce an invoice or a trial balance? How many iterations are needed to get it right–the needed output?

> What does it cost and how long does it take to negotiate a necessary design change, for safety reasons, and get it made and installed on your customers' premises?

> What does it cost and how long does it take to educate and train a sales trainee to become a sales representative?

> What is the total cost of a hip replacement operation?

> What does it cost to process an income tax return?

> What does it cost and how long does it take to get a legal opinion on the announcement of a new product?

> *Efficiency is a measure of how well your managers can organize and use their resources.*

If efficiency is low, the results will be poor. Cost and time will be needlessly high, with a corresponding negative impact on product or service *cost*-performance. This has a direct bearing on your pricing capability. Customers have absolutely no interest in what your costs are, but if your costs are high relative to competition, you cannot sustain a good relative *price*-performance, which really *does* interest your customers. Low efficiency of an invisible process can also adversely impact the performance of some customer-visible processes, where customers can directly make their own comparisons with your competitors.

Effectiveness
If efficiency is 'doing things right', then effectiveness is 'doing the right things'. You can be wonderfully efficient at transforming your inputs into invoices that are totally incomprehensible to the customer, incomplete and sent to the wrong address. Then you wonder why it is difficult to collect the money.

> Is the trial balance delivered on time? Is it understandable?

> Is the emergent sales representative well equipped to do the job, *to the total satisfaction of the customer*? (Offering products for sale is a very customer-visible process, and comparisons of the way it is done are made with the way your competitors do it.)

How long does it take to install the necessary engineering change? An hour? A day? A week? What is the impact on the customer's business because it takes so long? How many customer personnel are at risk because the customer decides to wait because it will take so long?

How long before the patient with the new hip can go home, walk, swim, play golf, whatever, and not have to come back for a new one for a very long time?

Is the income tax assessment based on all that is known, rather than just what the sender has decided to enter on the form?

How much potential market share will be lost because the legal people are refining their position to atomic purity, rather than making the right commercial assessment?

If effectiveness is low, you may well be internally efficient at producing results that do not meet the criteria of fitness for purpose. You may even be producing something that nobody wants.

Ford 're-engineered' the processes involved in paying its suppliers as part of a much wider-ranging effort on matching its requirements for parts with its production schedules. Instead of taking up to three months to make a manual match of 14 different items, the cheque is sent as soon as the goods are delivered. Only three items need be checked, by the computer system. As a result, Ford asked its suppliers to stop sending invoices. It has no further use for them.

Unfortunately, some suppliers were so locked into inflexible computer systems that they could not stop. So, they made the invoices anyway, then destroyed them! This is an example of a (probably) efficient invoicing process producing a completely worthless output.

Effectiveness is a measure of how well your managers understand and have negotiated the requirements of the people who use or depend on the outputs of their domain, that is, the requirements of their internal and external customers.

To know whether you are effective, you need to have the humility to ask *them*.

Employee satisfaction

This is a measure of how enthusiastically the managers' personnel want to play their manager's particular game. Managers can have the most superb strategies and plans, technologies, premises and so on in the world, but if their people do not participate enthusiastically, the results will be impacted.

Employee satisfaction is a measure of your managers' ability to motivate their personnel. It is one indicator of their actual or potential leadership qualities.

The ability to secure scarce or vital resources

Get the wrong data and you will make wrong invoices, or spend time chasing around the place for information to get the trial balance right. All this adds cost and time.

The people in Personnel might send you perfectly qualified candidates for sales training, but without the right instructors, technology, product, customer and competitor information, you will fail. Poorly equipped sales representatives will be let loose, despite their excellent potential.

Have you got the right surgical and nursing skills, the necessary technology, the beds? Are you so short of resources that the patients arrive too late for you to be able to do a really fine job?

How accurate is the installed interface information, which is needed by your designers to enable effective and fast installation of the necessary change? Do you know where *all* the potentially dangerous machines are installed?

If your legal people are fighting their way through mountains of paper, ancient and modern, no wonder their report is late. Maybe they need on-line access to legal information resources (like your competitors have?), the European Community legislation and so on.

In 1979, one of us was running a course in computer fundamentals for some senior managers. One of the things we showed was an on-line enquiry system for rummaging through text databases. Completely unstructured searches could be made on the occurrence of any word, or combination of words, for example. Engineering abstracts, pharmaceutical abstracts, abstracts from the business press, like the *Harvard Business Review*, the *Financial Times*, *The Wall Street Journal*, and so on could be searched. This is commonplace stuff now, but it was quite exotic in 1979.

We explained that you could also get on-line access to the latest European Community legislation, in text form. One of the participants was the general manager for Honda, Europe. As a Japanese among Europeans, he had been very quiet all week. When he saw this demonstration, he became quite excited. We later asked him why. He said, 'If I know about the different legislation changes sooner than my competitors, I may be able to take a competitive advantage'. He viewed this information as a critical business resource.

How strange that none of the European executives saw it this way.

The ability of your managers to secure scarce or vital resources is another measure of their negotiating skills, and this includes negotiating with you, too.

The skills of negotiation are becoming of critical importance as enterprises move to the looser, team-working, cross-functional, peer-to-peer organizations we discussed in Part 1, 'The changing middle management job'.

The ability to manage change

There may be excellence in terms of the first four factors, but this last one is the killer. Nothing is more important to modern enterprises than their effectiveness in coping with change.

Good *managers* can only work effectively in an environment of continual change (or else get an administrator). When there is this atmosphere of change, good managers can discover new combinations of opportunities. They will make change a normal way of life and continually challenge the status quo, even though today's results are good. This does not mean continual reorganization of the management structure. That would simply lead to a lot of thrashing around with little opportunity to deliver results. It is a matter of mental attitude, plus the ability to *implement* change.

How quickly can you react to a change of customer address so that the next invoice goes to the right place at the right time, or is it normal to take three or four months to do this? (Added cost for your enterprise. Added cost, and frustration, for your customer.)

How quickly can you modify your sales training to recognize a new competitor, a new market-place opportunity, new techniques, new technologies?

How well can your managers cope with changes in organization structure, merging of business units and so forth? How well can your managers handle a change of leadership when you move on?

Acquiring a new customer is a desirable example of change. How well do you do it, *from the customer's perspective*? The magazine *Art News* is not alone in saying, 'Allow six weeks for your first copy to be mailed'. What on earth goes on that it has to take six weeks? How many enthusiastic prospects cool off when they read this?

Your managers' ability to manage change is a measure of their ability to survive in the new, more competitive, less structured business environment.

It is another measure of leadership; of their fitness to be promoted, to do *your* job, perhaps.

If you replace 'employee satisfaction' with 'manager satisfaction', this list of factors can be applied to you as a middle manger. You *also* have to be efficient, effective, secure critically needed resources for your domain, manage change, change and more change, *and* have highly motivated managers.

We shall be giving you some tools to help you to do this.

CHECK-LIST 5   The quality of your managers today

You know something about your managers now, as a result of the earlier check-lists, and the managers all differ from one another.

Here again is the list of factors impacting their results:

- efficiency
- effectiveness
- employee satisfaction
- ability to secure scarce or vital resources
- ability to manage change.

Where are your manager's individual strengths and weaknesses on these critical factors?

Make an assessment for each of your managers, using a scale of A to E for each factor where

A = Excellent
B = Good
C = Fair
D = Bad
E = You really do not know

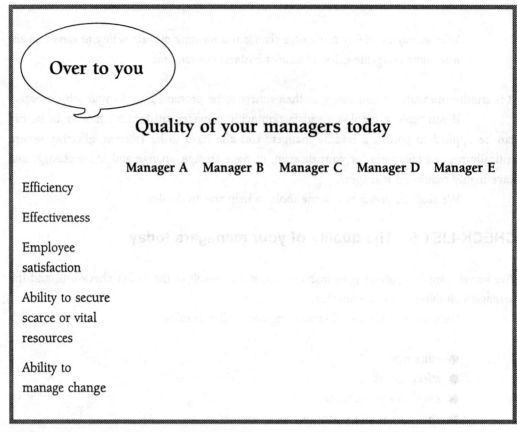

Over to you

Quality of your managers today

	Manager A	Manager B	Manager C	Manager D	Manager E
Efficiency					
Effectiveness					
Employee satisfaction					
Ability to secure scarce or vital resources					
Ability to manage change					

From Check-list 4, you know (roughly, at least)

- the most critical business processes in your domain, that is, those whose excellence will have the biggest impact on Total Quality/Total Competitiveness/Total Effectiveness
- the current quality of these processes.

Now from Check-list 5, you also know (roughly, at least)

- the current quality of your individual managers.

'Roughly, at least' is not good enough, but you are already better informed and better prepared than are most middle managers today. But you need to do a lot more work to refine your knowledge of these things. The following tools will help you to do this, in addition to helping you directly with your other stewardship processes. (Now do a self-assessment. How good are *you* at each of these factors? The aim of this book is to help you to manage your own improvement, too.)

Two important tools

Now you should know where you need at least to *start* focusing attention, on your managers as well as on your own development. We continue to concentrate here on your responsibility to improve the total quality of your managers, however. Part 6 is concerned with your own development.

Tool 1: monthly reviews

Properly done, these will help you to keep close to your managers and them close to you, but not so close that you get in each other's way.

Monthly review meetings should be held with each manager, individually. They serve to keep you informed and updated regularly, without bothering your managers all the time. Unless they need you, keep out of the way. As their management skills improve, and your leadership qualities develop, they will know when they really need you.

Be prepared in the early days for them to think they need your help when they really do not. Equally, you must beware of the opposite situation, early on, where a manager really *does* need your help, but either does not recognize it or, for some reason, does not choose to involve you.

Monthly review meetings are a good forum for flushing these situations out. And a monthly sequence is probably often enough to prevent any long-term damage being done. Organize and run them well, and soon your managers will recognize the out-of-line situations that really *do* need your unscheduled involvement. Remember, too, that in 'macho' cultures, a manager will tend not to ask for help or seek support.

Allow sufficient time for the review meeting to be thorough, and keep to it. Your managers will soon know that you are serious about the importance of the reviews. They will need to put a lot of effort into preparing for each review and on the discipline needed to cover all items on the agenda in the available time. You will rapidly lose credibility and respect (and leadership) as soon as you say, 'Sorry, I can only give you half an hour today. I have to go to …'.

Try to maintain a fixed date and time for the review meetings. Your managers and their people will become accustomed to the slot in the diaries and will plan around it. Equally, other colleagues will soon get the message that you are regularly not available at those times.

Of course, your managers should feel free to come to you at any time, but with a fixed, regular review meeting, all but urgent questions can be saved and deliberated on before being placed before you. Besides, many problems will solve themselves during the 'maturing' period.

A fixed agenda gives structure to the meeting and should enable effective allocation of time for each item. A useful agenda structure is as follows:

- personnel matters
- business issues
- concerns
- activities since last meeting
- plans for next period.

It is tempting to have exactly the reverse order. Then you may find that too much time is spent on the events and problems of the past few days and what will happen next. Personnel matters may be confined to a few sentences at the end: 'No staff problems?', 'Anything particular happening in your group?'

Many questions concerning personnel must be decided by you and your managers—appointments, movements, development activities, problems and so forth. You must keep *your* immediate manager informed, of course, but the final decision will normally be yours, rarely going above your level.

Personnel issues really must have this prominent position in the monthly review. Pay particular attention to:

- changes in the manager's group
- development of successors to managers
- development of successors to other key positions.

You will find that starting with personnel matters will raise questions that may not otherwise have emerged or may have been overlooked. Examples might range from the workload of the group to the need to plan for re-entry of an employee returning from maternity leave in two months' time. Personnel questions will be dealt with properly and not by last-minute improvisations while you both prepare to dash off to other meetings.

You should also explore how each manager's group works as a unit, both internally and with other groups, yours and elsewhere, within and beyond the boundary of the enterprise. You can contribute much value to this part of the meeting because you have a much broader overview and perspective.

Do not worry that insufficient time will remain to talk about the future and the business issues. For the first one or two meetings, there may be a feeling of rush and untidiness at the end, but you must demand that your managers come well prepared. It also means *you* have to be well-prepared—prepared to listen attentively and ask the right questions; no tedious monologues. The feeling of time pressure will quickly ensure they do it better next time, or it will signal something to you about their management quality.

Encourage your managers to spend time on the reviews of issues and not concerns. The difference is simple. An issue is something where the manager has done everything possible, but the problem or whatever has not been resolved. A concern, however, often represents an earlier stage. The manager has plans for further actions to resolve the problem or exploit the opportunity. If the manager does not succeed, the concern may evolve into an issue, which it is appropriate to put before you, either during your monthly review or immediately, if it is something urgent.

Tool 2: the management committee
This is a regular meeting, called by you, where all your managers are present. It must be perceived as being valuable to all of them. However, it is fraught with danger, particularly if there is little or no obvious interdependence between your managers and their individual groups.

The biggest danger is sullen boredom on the part of the people who are under pressure (from you) to deliver results. The solution is to *deal only with topics where everyone should have an interest* (if you believe that they should have an interest, and they manifestly do not, the failure is yours).

Depending on the strength and the nature of their interdependencies, the meetings can be very short or correspondingly longer. Either way, the agenda is under your control and you have to ensure that every minute of it is filled with value for all. The worst thing you can do is allow it to degenerate into a series of dialogues between you and one other manager.

Topics of common interest might include the following.

- Questions concerning common goals and activities for reaching *your* goals.
- Questions of cooperation and information flow *between* groups.
- Information flows from *outside* the groups. You may be able to find commonalities here that can be consolidated. Then *you* can negotiate, from your more senior position, for better quality and terms, for example, on behalf of everyone with the common need. Often, such information originates in another part of the enterprise—from another function, division or from corporate headquarters, for example. Your senior position should make it easier for you to deliver what is needed, and this means a greater recognition of your leadership qualities (clearly, this also applies to any other resource, not just information).
- How well do your managers need to be informed about each other? What is going on in neighbouring groups? Any bright ideas to help?

Then there is the social value, the importance of being a member of this team—your management committee.

Often you will find that your managers are not familiar with each other's areas. Your management committee provides an excellent opportunity to overcome this, to the benefit of all. A brief (ten-minute) presentation by one of your managers at each management committee meeting should not only be revealing to all, it might also provoke discussion of mutual benefit. You must ensure that these presentations explain *what* the manager is doing (the goals, issues, problems and so on) and that they are *not* descriptions of what a marvellous job is being done by the particular manager.

The agenda is yours. You must create a good working climate in your management committee. Every participant must agree to spend time on it and use the time actively. So, it is your responsibility to work on the common goals.

There is evidence that this is what managers really want to do anyway. Bo Mattsson, at the Gothenburg School of Economics, presented six case studies of how management teams work, as part of his doctoral thesis. One of his findings was that many teams spend their time on operational and short-term matters. The team members, however, indicated that they would have preferred to have more strategic discussions, focused on the common development of their business.

The management committee should also be a powerful development tool. New managers in particular can learn a lot from their more experienced colleagues, in an environment, moreover, where you are in control.

When your managers say, 'We really know too little about the rest of the department', it is a good sign. When your managers start saying 'we' instead of 'I', you will know it is beginning to work. You have begun to build a team.

The case of the leapfrogged manager

Then, suddenly, just when you think things are beginning to run smoothly, you get an unpleasant surprise.

One of your managers is called Martin. David, a member of Martin's group, calls at your office. Clearly, David is deeply concerned about something. You ask him in. He immediately tells you he cannot put up with Martin as his manager any longer, and it seems that he is not alone. He claims that several other people in the group feel the same way.

This is serious. You ask for more details. David unburdens himself to you.

The gist of it is this, from David's perspective.

Martin is not even *acceptable* as a manager.

He is almost never available; always travelling, going to seminars, meetings and so forth.

When he *is* available, there is never time to discuss anything except Martin's problems.

He has favourites. They get all the interesting work, the business trips and so on. The rest of his people get promises once a year at appraisal and counselling time—a gross misnomer in David's opinion.

Martin promises things will improve, but nothing ever happens.

Martin is either completely unaware of what he is doing to his group or he *is* aware, but cannot or will not change.

David himself suggests one possible solution: he leaves the company or he is transferred. He also says, 'but why should I? This is no fault of mine! I know I'm doing a good job. I like my work and the people in the group. *Martin* is the one who should leave. That's why I've come to you, to ask you to do something about it.'

The situation has apparently been smouldering on for a long time. David claims that he (and others) have raised these issues directly with Martin—his attitudes, unfulfilled promises and so forth—but Martin just does not seem to hear. You also discover that David is not there as a formal spokesman of the group, but some of the others know he has come to see you and they support him.

This problem will not go away. You assure David that you will look into it and you will get back to him in a week. You thank him for drawing your attention to the situation. He leaves.

Notice that this problem could not have occurred when you were a first-line manager. By its nature, it is specific to middle and top managers. The important principle is this:

> **When someone bypasses one of your managers and comes directly to**
> **you, deal with the case seriously, correctly and as swiftly as possible.**
> **Demonstrate your support for all the parties concerned.**

What are you going to do now?

We shall explore some possible approaches to this situation, but this is all. There will be no clear, pat solution at the end of it because Martin and David are not real people in a real situation. They do not exist. However, if this happens to you tomorrow, *you* will have to find a good solution. Yours *are* real people. The principles outlined here should help you to accomplish a good solution.

First, what would a good solution look like? What are the criteria of a good solution? Here are some suggestions that we shall use for this particular case.

Criteria of a good solution for the Martin case

1 Normal business is not impacted. We must be able to run as usual.

2 Everyone concerned acknowledges that the solution is positive; an improvement.

3 Where motivation is low today, it is high tomorrow.

There is one easy solution, of course. You may even have seen it happen. Promote Martin! The results of this would be that:

- the group gets a new manager (maybe David?)
- Martin is happy
- the group is happy—with a small question about the 'favourites'
- business is not unduly disturbed.

The criteria are pretty well satisfied, are they not?

However, this only solves your local problem and it may be bad for the business as a whole. Suppose David is right. If so, does Martin *deserve* promotion? Does his next group deserve to get *him*? Should he be the manager of *anybody*?

At present, you do not know whether David is right, half right or totally wrong.

What do you know about Martin?

You *do* know something about Martin, from the work you did in Part 2 'Acclimatizing to the new role', and you have made a *preliminary* assessment of his quality against the key factors bearing on results. For Martin, it might look like this:

- efficiency   B (good)
- effectiveness   B (good)
- employee satisfaction   E (don't know)
- ability to secure resources   B (good)
- ability to manage change   E (don't know).

Now, though, you can change the 'E' against employee satisfaction to 'D' (bad).

David may be totally wrong about Martin, but David's level of satisfaction is very low. One is enough. Please resist the temptation to write B/D, for example, meaning 'good in parts'. You should not accept that employee satisfaction is good until *all* of them acknowledge it to be good.

Now, there is something additional that you know about Martin. In a well-managed group, the manager *does* know the level of employee satisfaction (if you can't measure it, you can't manage it). It is an indisputable fact that David (at least) is highly dissatisfied. If Martin did *not* know, he is at fault. If he *did* know, but did not choose to put such a long-lasting and unsolved issue (this is not a mere concern!) in front of you, he is *still* at fault. It should have featured high on the agenda of your monthly review with him. It is certainly not in the category of something that would go away during the maturing period between review meetings.

In addition, there is some support for David's discomfort in that you started with two big 'don't knows'—employee satisfaction and ability to cope with change. On the other hand, Martin *does* appear to be able to deliver results, probably the basis for your preliminary 'B' ratings for efficiency, effectiveness and ability to secure resources, and you have not personally noticed any major motivation problems. Nor has anyone else brought them to your notice.

However you did notice how difficult it was to get a little time to talk with him to address the issues in 'Acclimatizing to the new role' of Part 2.

The fact is, you just do not know enough.

You will have to discuss this with Martin, soon. What other sources of information can you explore before then, to confirm or deny all or part of what David told you?

- Your predecessor. An obvious choice, if you can make contact, but do not be surprised if this line is not fruitful. It is a little like asking your predecessor to admit to not having done a good job. However, it is worth trying.
- Your boss. Your own boss may not be able to give you much information, but the involvement and support of your boss may be essential in providing a solution, so try.
- Other members of Martin's group. Yes, but beware! Suppose David is *wrong*. You can quickly and permanently alienate your relationship with Martin by bypassing him, this time in the opposite direction.

  Have you a natural reason to get in touch with people in Martin's group? A project status meeting? A special issue that you want to review or discuss? You might be considering having lunch meetings, for example, with small groups of people from all parts of your domain. Start with Martin's. You will have to plan a *very* careful approach, and be *very* sensitive to all kinds of subtle verbal and non-verbal signals.

  Do not jump to conclusions if you learn nothing. Most people are cautious about criticizing their manager in public.
- Outsiders. Who has left Martin's group in the past year or two? Maybe you know one or two of them personally. In any case, providing you can contact them, they may be able to throw some light on the matter. If you *can* contact your predecessor, ask why they left (but maybe your predecessor did not hold

'departure interviews' when people left; you *must*).

It is too early to consider the option of using an outside consultant, say. Martin would very quickly assume (correctly) that you were prying.

Please add other sources of information that you think could be explored, *without prejudicing a good solution*. There is not much chance of finding clear evidence. All you can hope is to confirm or deny *some* of what David has told you. This is not an exact science!

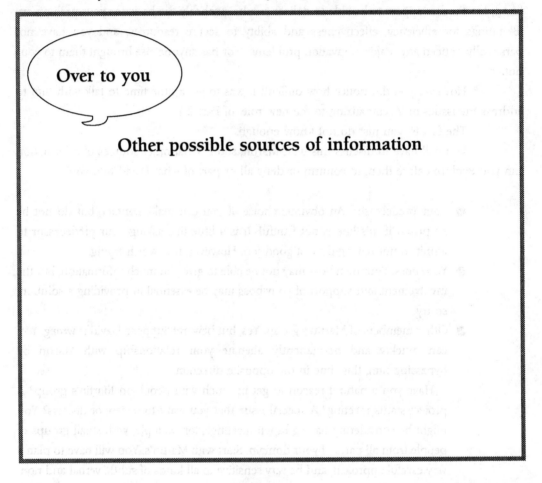

Over to you

Other possible sources of information

Promoting Martin would be wrong. For the same reasons, a sideways move would be wrong. You have not yet identified the real problem. Such a move would merely fix the symptoms rather than the cause. Let us consider some alternative approaches before you have your meeting with Martin.

If David is right?

Either Martin is aware of his shortcomings and accepts the description or you have sufficient knowledge that there really is no doubt. The next question is, do you believe that it is possible for Martin to change his ways in relation to managing his people? If the answer is 'yes', then you must discuss and plan for his development.

It will not be easy. Considering the criteria of a good solution, this could work, but *only* if David and the rest feel confident that Martin can make this change. Without such confidence, the odds are against you.

If David is right, you will probably need to be heavily involved to gain this confidence. Martin has lost a lot of credibility. He will not be regarded as being trustworthy. You may have to give the group some kind of guarantee, your personal commitment. Martin has to deliver an early success. You have to stick to your commitment and deliver a visibly improved Martin.

On the other hand, if Martin does *not* have the ability or willingness to change, he quite simply is not the right person for the job. You then have to find out under what circumstances he *could* be a successful manager. The opportunities are certainly limited, but he must have learned *something* at all those seminars he has attended.

He may have to revert to a professional status. An indicator of this might be that you find he is neglecting his management tasks in favour of getting professionally involved in the detail of operations. Maybe this is where his strength and happiness lie? If so, this satisfies the criteria. The group will probably welcome a new manager, carefully selected and prepared by you (those 'favourites' have to be brought back into the team). Business will not be unduly affected. The solution is acceptable to all.

If Martin is dissatisfied with reverting to a professional status, though, some criteria will be met, but not all. You will have a former manager who is disgruntled, to say the least.

If David is wrong?

In this case, it is no longer a question of how to deal with Martin. You have to handle David.

Why is he wrong? He may be playing games, exaggerating, trying to gain some personal advantage, trying to exploit the fact that you are quite new to the job. Maybe he 'tried it on' with your predecessor and was rejected.

He is more likely to be wrong because of misunderstanding or lack of knowledge, however. He is probably not fully aware of priorities within the group, the responsibilities of his colleagues and so on. There may be very good reasons for some of them travelling more than others—meetings they need to attend as part of their work, within the company and beyond, with suppliers, customers, strategic alliance partners, trade, government and professional bodies, for example. It may be that his expectations of Martin are too high. Martin may not be perfect, but who is? (But you *do* know he could be *better*.)

If David really has got the group's interests at heart and is honestly interested in having the situation corrected (but still is wrong about Martin), you are on common ground and can correct the situation. There seems a good chance that this is David's attitude. After all,

David came to you of his own volition with this sensitive problem. He might just as easily have said, 'I have accepted a better job with the competition, but I want you to know the real reasons for my leaving'.

If David *does* have a positive attitude, you can jointly address one issue at a time. It really is Martin's job, but, in the circumstances, you have to be the visible and committed catalyst. Martin might need some coaching from you, initially, and you should be present at the first few meetings between Martin and David to monitor progress towards a positive and constructive atmosphere, and to demonstrate your commitment to a good outcome. It certainly fits the criteria of a good solution, but do not underestimate the difficulties. This has been building up for some time.

David may be only partly right (or wrong), of course. You will know more after you have explored all your avenues of information. Whatever your conclusions, you cannot move forwards without the willing participation of both Martin and David.

You said you would get back to David in a week. This is the time to let him know what you have found out and to sell to him the need for a joint approach to a solution. When he first came to see you, he may well have emphatically refused the opportunity to discuss this with you and Martin together, out of fear of reprisals from Martin. Now, after you have demonstrated your concern and commitment, he may feel more trust and confidence in you.

You must also have your meeting with Martin. Prepare for it very carefully, based on what you now know. The meeting has to be formal and structured. This is not just any old chat. Make it clear at the beginning that, *regardless* of his opinions, he has an employee satisfaction problem. You have to make it equally clear that you must have an improvement and that you will support him in making this improvement.

Be prepared for strong reactions, particularly if Martin is still unaware of being bypassed by David.

'Why didn't you come to me directly instead of conspiring with others behind my back?'

'Have you any complaints about my results?'

My former manager *never* said anything like this. You've only been here a couple of months and you tell me I'm not doing my job!'

'With my massive workload, and all these changes going on, how do you expect me to keep on top of *everything*?'

and so on.

Try to anticipate these outbursts and prepare your responses. They should be responses that lower the temperature and consistently lead to Martin accepting that something is not right, and that you and he (and David) must sort it out together.

Then, describe your action plan. Now may be the time to suggest an impartial outsider, a management consultant, perhaps. Martin may jump at the offer—after all, the problem *must* be solved—or he may express his determination to sort things out entirely by himself. This is not an option now, however—you *have* to be actively involved, at least initially.

The climate of trust

The case of Martin and David illustrates not only the *need* for middle managers, but also how the nature of the job has changed.

The *need* is there because someone has to sort it out or it will get worse of its own accord. Once a situation like this reaches a critical mass, it is very difficult to stop. Conversation among the disaffected members of the group increasingly moves from affairs of the job to a concentration on the (to them) increasingly bizarre and unfair behaviour of Martin—'You'll never guess where he's gone now!', and so forth. Imagine the consequences if you do nothing about it after David's visit. Martin seems to be unable to sort it out spontaneously. David might provide a solution, of course, by resigning. He might take not only his own skills, knowledge and experience, but also those of some equally disaffected employees. This is not a good solution.

The middle manager's job has *changed*; from the giving of instructions to one of enabling and supporting. For Martin and David, it is a case of enabling the right solution to start, then supporting it all the way to a good conclusion.

Passing it on to the Personnel Department, or whatever, is no solution. This particular buck stops with you.

Often, the situation is not so clear-cut and direct as in the Martin and David case. You will more usually be given hints and heavily disguised leads, often dressed as jokes or wisecracks. If you miss these subtle messages or underestimate their importance (easily done) the personnel concerned will draw the conclusions that you:

- are not interested
- do not understand
- do not care
- are always on the side of the manager.

The two tools we have presented so far—monthly reviews and your management committee—failed to reveal the Martin and David problem. However, it *should* have come out in your monthly review with Martin. It *would* have come out if you had had the time to create a climate of trust. It is a component of leadership that does take time to develop, so start now. A climate of trust is essential if you are to perform your stewardship role effectively. Moreover, when this trust extends to all personnel, important hints and messages need not be so heavily disguised.

Reflect for a few minutes on what it is like when there is a climate of trust.

Over to you

The climate of trust

What does it feel like?

What are its characteristics?

How do you recognize it when you have it?

What do you need to do to create it and sustain it?

Some attributes of a climate of trust follow. They do not stand alone, the excellence of one depending on the excellence of others.

Predictability–being right

We trust people who are predictable. You have to be able to predict outcomes with a high probability of being right. This is the essence of leadership.

Predictability is strongly dependent on *clear communications*; being well-informed about a wide range of operating decisions that are made all over the enterprise, and beyond, among customers, suppliers, alliance partners, government and so on.

This need to be *informed* about operations is not in conflict with the basic principle of not getting *involved* in operational details. It simply means that you know what is going on. Of course, it includes your desktop computer, capable of accessing all kinds of information within and beyond the enterprise. Of possibly greater importance to you, however, is your own *personal* network. (We shall be saying a lot more about your personal network in Part 6, 'Maintaining your own development'.)

Being right creates an air of confidence; confidence in yourself, confidence of your managers in you. It manifests itself in your ability to develop the talents of your managers. If you doubt your own ability to improve them, you will expect correspondingly less *of* them. You will treat them with less confidence and it will be transparently obvious that you are doing so.

Clear communications

Clear communications are needed *from* you so that everyone you work with knows your priorities and expectations. People cannot assess your predictability (remember, *they* do the assessment!) unless they know what you are predicting. If you do not make your priorities and expectations known to your peers, your subordinates and your bosses, they will have to guess, and they will be wrong.

Clear communications are needed *towards* you so that you can know that what you sent out was accurately received *and accepted*. Clear communications towards you are equally important in order for you to know exactly what is going on. Initially, no matter how strongly you say that you encourage honest feedback–and you mean it–people will rarely believe you *really* mean it.

Do not underestimate the difficulty your managers will have in being totally honest with you about their own problems and weaknesses. This is particularly true in the early days after your appointment. After all, you are probably viewed as having a strong influence on their future careers. Perhaps this was at the root of Martin's problem in his relationship with his previous manager, and now with you, the new one.

The good news is, this is a virtuous circle. The more you build the climate of trust, the more honest and open will be the feedback you receive (but, as we said earlier, beware of people who only bring you good news).

You should maintain and expand your personal network. You have to be constantly foraging about, inside the enterprise and beyond. Information really is power.

Relevance

Your managers (and their people) have to feel that what you are trying to do is important to them as individuals. You have to translate and communicate the organization's vision, goals or whatever in a manner that stresses the values of your audience. So, you have to know what these values are (more links to clear communications) and you have to involve them. Unless your managers have a hand in formulating the strategy for their part of the enterprise, they will not understand what the enterprise is trying to do and they will be correspondingly less likely to fall in smoothly with the plans.

Consistency

Predictability means getting the right results, consistently, of course. By consistency we mean that there is no ambiguity between your words and your actions. The worst remark you can overhear about yourself is 'speaking out of both sides of the mouth at the same time, as usual'.

When you say, 'We are going to be customer-driven from now on', for example, *you* have to be visibly customer-driven, too. *You* have to be seen to be spending a large portion of your time with customers, in this example, and your actions back at work have to reflect what you have learned from customers.

Beware of the vision ('we are going to be customer-driven') conflicting with the short-term pressures: 'Yes, I know that Harry, but you have to reduce service costs by ten per cent anyway', or, 'I don't care whether the customer really needs to order it this quarter or not, just get the order!' This sort of thing, understandably, leads to the 'both sides of the mouth at the same time' kind of perception.

There are ways in which service costs can be reduced without prejudicing customer satisfaction. Demonstrate your skill and leadership by exploring the possibilities together, as a team. Thereby, you maintain the integrity of your vision to be customer-driven, while delivering *jointly* a cost benefit to the enterprise.

How often do you cancel/postpone/shorten meetings with your managers (or anyone else)? Never mind the reasons! How often?

Fairness

Fairness relates to predictability, in a way. People know where they stand—there are no favourites, no discrimination for any reason. Success is recognized and rewarded, but you are not a 'soft touch'. When admonishment is called for, it is given without discrimination and accepted (even reluctantly) as justified.

You do not move the goalposts because someone has been spectacularly successful

An example is the sales quota 'adjustment' that takes place when a sales representative gets much more business than was originally expected. Such adjustments do *not* contribute to a climate of trust. If the sales quota (set by management) was too low, it is management's fault. If the sales representative worked hard, innovatively, or even was just plain lucky, pay the commission for goodness sake. Not only is it fair, it is a powerful motivator for the rest because they know you will keep your word when *they* succeed.

Fairness is particularly important when you divide your own goals among your managers. They may be tough goals, but they have to be seen as fair by all. If *they* are not satisfied with the 'contracts' that they have with you, unfair contracts will be promulgated to your managers' people. This can damage managements' credibility (the climate of trust) as well as the authority for your entire domain.

Visibility

You must mix with your managers and with their people to promote a spirit of teamwork. You are also the role model, demonstrating the values and policies of the enterprise. When someone like you picks up a piece of litter from a factory floor, for example, and puts it into a bin (rather than just stepping over it), people notice. You don't have to be theatrical about it, just pick it up. They will notice all right. Equally, when someone like you starts to tidy up the room after a meeting—cups, pieces of flipchart paper and so forth—your people will quickly realize that this is something they should do also. Quite often, sensitive or confidential information will be lying about after some meetings. Again, you can be an effective role model.

The mixing referred to above is partly how you will monitor what is really going on, of course, but the focus here is on your *personal* visibility.

Make your thought processes visible, too, by making it a normal practice to involve your managers in your own decision making and approvals. Your management committee is a good forum for starting this, but you must not abdicate from making decisions.

As you see, it will take time to build such a climate of trust. It is essential for you to have it, however, in order to do your job properly. No doubt you will also have noticed that everything we have discussed here will result in an enhancement of your qualities of *leadership*, too. This can only be a good thing.

You may recall from earlier management training, when you were a first-line manager, that one of the strengths of a good manager is good self-knowledge. How do you rate yourself today on the factors we have just examined for building a climate of trust? We do not claim that our list is complete, by the way, so please also rate yourself against any other factors that you believe to be important. Use the 'A' to 'E' scale again, where 'E' means you still do not know enough to rate yourself accurately. Then find out what you need to know.

Factor	Rating
Predictability–being right	
Clear communications	
Relevance	
Consistency	
Fairness	
Visibility	

Of course, it is equally important that your managers create a climate of trust. For this, your best contribution is to be a good role model.

Improving the Total Quality of management

Up to this point we have described some measures and tools, but nothing about how to address your key responsibility, that of *improving* the Total Quality of your managers. We shall summarize the measures and tools, then move on to making the improvements, that is, getting the results by which you will be judged and by which you will judge your managers.

You now know, at least roughly, the following.

- *Your most critical business processes and their current quality.* These are the activities within your domain of the enterprise for which excellence is essential if the highest quality outputs from it are to be delivered. You know which of them are customer-visible and which are normally invisible to customers. They will not all be excellent today. This means that your domain is not making its maximum possible contribution to Total Quality/Competitiveness/Effectiveness.

  Many other sources of literature, advice, expertise, consultancy and so on can be used to address the Total Quality opportunities in general. In this book, though, we are focusing on only *one* necessary condition for excellence of your processes: the excellence of management.

You now know, at least roughly, the following.

- *The quality attributes of your managers–their:*

—efficiency
—effectiveness
—employee satisfaction
—ability to secure resources
—ability to manage change.

Like your business processes, these will not all be excellent today, but, also like the processes, excellence is the *only* acceptable standard. (Remember, too, that they are the quality attributes of you as a manager.)

You also know that 'at least roughly' is not good enough. Two tools provide you with part of the means necessary to refine your knowledge and monitor progress towards excellence:

● *monthly reviews*—a means for monitoring individual managers
● your *management committee*—a means for monitoring your group, as a team.

Both of these are more than just monitoring devices, however. They are two of the channels you will use for your *clear communications*.

You also know the following.

● The *means necessary to build a climate of trust* are:

—predictability—being right
—clear communications
—relevance
—consistency
—fairness
—visibility.

Use these to create the necessary conditions for your stewardship of the management resource to be excellent. Whereas this is a tool for *you* to improve yourself, notice also that you can apply it to your managers. They *also* have to build a climate of trust. There is a question mark over Martin's achievements here, for example.

Ways in which to develop managers

Now you can move on. You know where you are starting from, 'at least roughly'.

Check-list 6 is quite a long list of techniques for developing managers. You will have experienced some of them yourself. Please add others that you believe are missing from the list, but useful to have.

CHECK-LIST 6   A management development tool-box

☐ Harnessing the manager's own insight and drive to improve.

☐ Special job objectives aimed at a particular developmental aspect.

☐ Special assignments, task forces and projects.

☐ Job rotation.

☐ Use of consultants when breaking new ground–procedures, technology, systems, for example.

☐ Introduction to the enterprise's history and values (for managers recruited from outside).

☐ Formal management education programmes, workshops, seminars and so forth, such as:

- ■ university, business school

- ■ broadening education, to expand perspectives on international issues, social issues, the environment, cultural differences and so forth

- ■ professional education

- ■ management development programmes

- ■ how the enterprise operates–processes, procedures, relationships

- ■ personal development.

☐ Books, trade journals, abstracts, magazines, on-line information sources.

☐ Professional and trade organizations, participation in meetings, conferences, working parties.

☐ Participation in local government, charities, sports organizations and so forth.

☐ Working in other parts of the enterprise or with customers, suppliers, alliance partners, government agencies and so forth.

☐ You as a role model.

☐ Delegation of some of your tasks, as a formal development activity.

☐ Being your deputy:

- ■ temporarily, when you are away

- ■ permanently, on specific committees, for example.

◻ On-the-job training—coaching from you (by coaching, we mean something that you and the manager have formally agreed to be a development activity. You plan it together. You support the manager throughout the activity and you give appropriate feedback at the end.

◻ Contacts with top management.

This is a large tool-box, filled with special tools, some of which are rather expensive. Some are more appropriate for one situation than another. Most of them are on-the-job training. You need a structure for choosing the most appropriate tools, for getting the right fit for any situation. We shall be dipping into this tool-box soon as a means to help Martin, for example. First, we shall describe a structure for planning management development. Then, the right tools can be chosen. However, if the right tool is not in the tool-box, you will have to find one, or design it yourself.

Planning management development

The purpose of the worksheets that follow is to enable you to identify which aspects of a manager's skills need to be improved, either to correct a deficiency for the manager's current role or to prepare the manager for some future role.

There is a very large number of items to consider. Although we say 'the manager must...' on every one of them, the paragon of management virtue, with a tick against every one of them, probably does not exist in reality. The idea is to provide a structure for your own thinking. In any given situation, for any given manager, you should be able to sort out the 'nice to have' items from those that are really important for the new job or for solving the current problem.

You may have selected a particular manager to represent your enterprise on a National Standards committee. The manager has shown promise and is ready for a more broadening external experience.

We shall use the first worksheet to illustrate the approach. This one looks at 'our arena'. It is to evaluate how well a manager is aware (or needs to be aware) of the larger picture concerning the relationship between the manager's domain and the outside world. What potential opportunities or threats are there resulting from external forces, for example? (Notice that the worksheets are a quality *measurement* tool as well as a tool for management development.)

Name of Manager: A. N. Other
Our arena

The manager must

☐ Understand general *external factors* that influence the enterprise and the manager's own area of responsibility.

☐ Understand *international developments* (in technology, legislation, society, business structure and so on) that affect our enterprise and our industry.

☐ Understand *national developments* (technology, legislation and so on) that affect our enterprise and our industry.

☐ Have a *broad view* of the manager's own area of responsibility.

☐ Have a good *network* in related organizations.

☐ Have good personal contacts with *external customers*.

☐ Be able to *represent* our enterprise to the outside world.

Knowing the nature of the work and the attributes of the manager, you have chosen three areas as being key for development:

- understand developments in the country
- have personal contacts in industry and government bodies
- be able to represent us well to the outside world.

Now you know the result you want and the changes needed in this particular manager. It is time to look in your tool-box (see Check-list 6, page 78) to identify the *means* to achieve these changes. The complete set of 13 worksheets that comprises Check-list 7 follows.

CHECK-LIST 7   Worksheets for developing managers

Worksheet 1 Our arena

Name of manager:.....................

The manager must

☐ Understand *external factors* that influence the enterprise *and* the managers's own area of responsibility.

☐ Understand *international developments* (in legislation, society, culture, technology, economics and so forth) that affect our enterprise and our industry.

☐ Understand *national developments* that affect our enterprise and our industry.

☐ Have a *broad view* of their own development and how it relates to the external world.

☐ Have an effective *network* in related organizations.

☐ Have good personal contacts with *external customers* and *suppliers*.

☐ Be able to *represent* our enterprise and the manager's own area of responsibility to the outside world.

Key areas for this manager/this job

Worksheet 2 Our enterprise

The manager must

☐ Understand our enterprise's *culture* and interpret it to the manager's people.

☐ Act in accordance with the enterprise's *values and policies*.

☐ Understand the *organization* and the role of the manager's group.

☐ Understand the *strategies* as they affect the manager's group and interpret them for the manager's people.

☐ Understand *developments within the enterprise* (technologies, business, products, services and so forth).

☐ Have an effective *network* within the enterprise.

☐ Be able to use the *decision regimes* within the enterprise:

- ■ budgets
- ■ investments
- ■ hiring
- ■ appointments and so forth.

Key areas for this manager/this job

Worksheet 3 Business sense

The manager must

☐ Understand the enterprise's *objectives/mission/vision/goals* and so on.

☐ Know the *internal and external customers* of the group, their needs and any significant changes in needs.

☐ Know the *internal and external suppliers* of the group, and how changes may affect their ability to deliver needed inputs.

☐ Base *proposals and decisions* on a broad view and good business sense.

☐ Know how to evaluate *risks* and consider them when making decisions.

Key areas for this manager/this job

Worksheet 4 Basic management responsibilities

The manager must

☐ Control the use of normal *working hours* and overtime, within legal limits.

☐ Plan and grant *holidays* and *leave of absence* in accordance with legislation and policies.

☐ Use correct *terms of employment* for full-time, part-time and temporary employees.

☐ Take full responsibility for *safety* and a good working environment.

☐ Control the *expenditure* of the group, according to budget.

☐ Make *salary adjustments* for staff, when required.

☐ Be able to use the *personnel programmes* of the enterprise.

Key areas for this manager/this job

Worksheet 5 Developing the business

The manager must

☐ Understand the *need for change*, what changes need to be made and be able to communicate the need effectively.

☐ *Take initiatives* within the manager's area of responsibility.

☐ *Create a climate* that encourages improvements and innovation.

☐ Drive *simplification* of methods and *stop doing* unimportant activities.

☐ Manage the *change processes* creatively and constructively.

Key areas for this manager/this job

Worksheet 6 Planning

The manager must

☐ *Organize* the group to meet the demands with available resources.

☐ Define *strategies* for the manager's area of responsibility.

☐ Formulate *operating plans*.

☐ *Plan projects* with objectives, activities, responsibilities and milestones.

☐ *Estimate and plan* needed resources.

☐ Propose a well-prepared *budget*.

☐ *Plan and assign tasks* on a daily or short-term basis.

☐ *Follow up* all plans regularly.

☐ *Involve* the manager's group in the planning process.

Key areas for this manager/this job

Worksheet 7 Relationships

The manager must

☐ Demonstrate an ability to *cooperate* well with people.

☐ Be able to work with *union representatives* in a correct and constructive manner.

☐ Represent *absent parties*, such as management towards personnel, and vice versa.

☐ Establish an environment of *teamwork* and team spirit in the group.

☐ Be able to *assess people* in relation to hiring, development, promotion.

☐ *Resolve conflicts* between people and groups.

Key areas for this manager/this job

Worksheet 8 Communication

The manager must

☐ Have a *vision* for the manager's area of responsibility and engage others in working towards it.

☐ Effectively *present* proposals, business cases and so forth to management, specialists, users or customers to reach the desired objectives—support, information, a decision and so on.

☐ Create an *environment* in which constructive criticism and new ideas thrive.

☐ *Understand* people by being a good observer and listener.

☐ *Explain* the background and reasons for decisions, guidance and so on.

☐ Be effective in holding hiring and other *interviews*.

☐ Conduct effective *meetings*.

☐ Find enterprise *information* and share it with the group.

☐ Keep the manager's group *informed*.

☐ Be a good *teacher*, transferring knowledge and skills to others.

☐ Be able to *negotiate* successfully to achieve agreeable results.

☐ Give constructive positive or negative *feedback* on performance.

☐ *Communicate sensitively* and well with people from different cultures.

Key areas for this manager/this job

Worksheet 9 Personal effectiveness

The manager must

☐ Set realistic and challenging *targets* and track progress.

☐ Define *quality* within the manager's domain and use quality targets.

☐ Follow up to ensure that activities are completed *on time*.

☐ Manage, review and control *projects*.

☐ Be able to initiate and lead effective *task forces*.

☐ Be able to *use resources* and expertise from other parts of the enterprise.

☐ Manage *own time* according to business priorities.

☐ *Delegate* tasks effectively.

☐ Not waste the time of *other people* (personnel, peers, management and so on).

☐ Encourage and promote the use of *productivity tools*.

☐ Run *productive meetings*.

☐ Effectively *introduce new members* to the group.

☐ Deal promptly with cases of *low performance*.

Key areas for this manager/this job

Worksheet 10 Personnel development

The manager must

☐ *Review and assess* competence, strengths and development potential of personnel.

☐ Be able to use a *range of methods* for developing people.

☐ Set realistic *development goals* and plan activities for reaching them.

☐ Review job performance and *coach for improvement*.

☐ Give constructive *feedback* on job performance.

☐ Use *delegation* as a means of developing personnel.

☐ Be an effective *coach* for the personnel.

Key areas for this manager/this job

Worksheet 11 Motivation

The manager must

☐ Understand what motivates *different people*.

☐ Understand *motivating and demotivating factors* for the people in the manager's group.

☐ *Create conditions* for job satisfaction and high motivation.

☐ *Inspire* personnel to work towards a shared vision or common goals.

☐ *Involve* personnel in defining job objectives.

☐ Make effective use of the *salary programme* as a motivating factor.

☐ Make effective use of the *award programme* as a motivating factor.

Key areas for this job/this manager

Worksheet 12 Formal education and experience

The manager must

☐ Have the appropriate *education level* for the job.

☐ Have the right *trade or professional qualifications* for this job.

☐ Have completed any *prerequisites*–complementary education or courses.

☐ Have appropriate *language skill.*

☐ Meet formal requirements of *previous experience.*

☐ Have received *management skills training.*

Key areas for this manager/this job.

Worksheet 13 Some personality factors

The manager must

☐ Have *analytical abilities* (be able to see patterns and priorities in complicated situations).

☐ Be *adaptable and flexible* (be able to accept new conditions and procedures, be willing to learn).

☐ Be *creative* (be able to see reality from different angles and find new ideas and solutions to problems).

☐ Be *decisive* (have the will and ability to make evaluations and take appropriate decisions).

☐ Have *implementation skills* (take responsibility for and ownership of decisions and so on, implement decisions and finish projects).

☐ Be *ambitious* (have a desire to succeed, to deliver needed results, and demand much of themselves and of others).

☐ have a capacity for *simultaneous processing* (be able to work with a number of different things at the same time).

☐ Be *stable and consistent* (be able to cope with stress, ambiguity, uncertainty, setbacks and still display balance and good judgement).

☐ Demonstrate *loyalty* (accept and act according to the enterprise's values, policies and decisions).

☐ Have *integrity* (take initiatives and act according to the manager's own convictions; have the courage to say 'no' when necessary).

☐ Be *positive* (have a constructive view and the will to contribute to reaching solutions and goals).

☐ Be *honest* (fulfil promises and make objective evaluations).

☐ *Have a sense of humour.*

☐ Be *open-minded* (have good self-knowledge and be prepared to acknowledge their own mistakes).

☐ Be genuinely *interested in people* (show personal involvement in the manager's people, their problems and their needs).

☐ Be *enthusiastic* (lead by example, distinguishing between genuine enthusiasm and messianic fanaticism).

☐ Give and deserve *trust* (create the conditions for open, honest and risk-free discussion; treat people fairly).

☐ Be an effective *role model* (demonstrate the above factors).

Key factors for this manager/this job

Using the management development worksheets

This is how we recommend you use the worksheets.

- Go through each worksheet and identify the most important attributes for the particular job.
- Consider the manager. Select which areas most need improvement, restricting yourself to the really critical ones.
- Decide the best way to achieve the desired results. Your 'Management development tool-box', Check-list 6, will help here (see page 78).

Each time you select a particular attribute as being important, pause, then ask yourself *why* you selected it. Is it simply a reflection of your own personal style? Were you thinking of someone else? A peer? Your predecessor? A former mentor? Be very careful that you do not use an old mould to shape a new manager. There are many ways of succeeding in any particular job. Are you exploiting the strengths of the manager, investing in the development of these strengths? Perhaps this would be better, for a given situation, than trying to correct some weaknesses.

Yes, the number of attributes is very large—over a hundred—and no doubt you will be able to add a few more. The intention is to provide a wide and deep selection so that nothing vital can escape your consideration. Yes, it will require hard concentration on your part—this is not easy work—but please remember not to try to 'boil the ocean', so to speak. The end product, your development plan, should be distilled to not more than, say, two improvement areas, but they are the key ones for this manager, today.

As usual, when you use the worksheets in practice, look also for things that are *not* there, then add them. This is not our final list, just our latest version. Regard it as your first version, the starting point from which to make your own additions.

Resist the temptation to throw the lists at a manager and say, 'Here. Do some self-assessment and we'll sort out some kind of development plan for you'. (What would Martin have chosen for himself?) Perhaps the manager has never before heard from you (or anyone else) what precisely the expectations of performance are. These worksheets are for *you* to use.

You have to look beneath the surface of your assessment of apparently poor performance before choosing the right development approach, however. Suppose you are concerned that one of your managers appears not to be good at presenting the views and decisions of top management.

Maybe it is due to lack of knowledge, not being aware which messages to identify with. Maybe the perception is that the messages are ambiguous. (This is *your* problem. You are the intermediary with top management—*clear communications*, remember?)

Maybe the manager is insecure in the role, identifying too strongly with the audience and not enough with the absent parties—representing management poorly when talking to the group; representing the group poorly when talking to management.

Maybe the manager is bad at prioritizing time—everything is done in a rush. Maybe the manager's people have too high an expectation of information and participation. Perhaps there are long-serving professionals in the group who are strong, articulate and have a better information network via the rumour mill.

Just looking at the *surface* symptoms of not being good at presenting the views and decisions of top management might indicate that the manager would benefit from participation in a workshop on presentation skills, but this is not necessarily the best solution here.

So, you have to look beyond the surface symptoms and make an accurate diagnosis before you can prescribe the right remedy.

An old doctor was taking his very young new assistant on his rounds. At the first house, the old doctor took the patient's pulse and temperature. Then he said, 'You are improving well, Mr Johnson, but you must drink rather less alcohol. In moderation, it is no bad thing, but you are taking too much'. Outside, the young doctor expressed his amazement. 'How on earth did you know he drank a lot, simply by taking his pulse and temperature?' The old doctor replied, 'You have to look beneath the surface. Did you notice me drop my thermometer case? It gave me a chance to look around under the bed. There were two empty whisky bottles. Simple. Do you want to take the next case?'

At the next house, the young assistant duly measured pulse and temperature, having first dropped the thermometer case. Then he said, 'You are doing fine, Mrs Brown. And religion is a fine thing. In your case, though, when it becomes all-pervasive and dominates your life, it may impede your progress towards full physical health. Moderation, Mrs Brown'.

Outside, the old doctor was very impressed. 'That was brilliant! What on earth did you see under the bed?' 'Oh. The bishop', the young assistant replied.

We repeat. The diagnosis must be *accurate*.

You may be surprised to find, for example, that one of your managers is coaching the local basketball team. You are surprised because your perception of this person is that they are poor at making decisions, always coming to you before taking any action. Here is a successful leader outside the office, but a shrinking violet at work. Find out why, then fix it. Exploit the manager's real strengths, and don't look too narrowly at their present job. Think about the potential for development to do other, more challenging jobs.

Try using the worksheets for Martin. This is not an easy case to start with, but there is no risk—Martin and David do not exist, remember. You have only a very incomplete picture, so you can only begin to *approach* a proper analysis, but you now know as much about it as we do. Let us assume there is some truth in what David has told you, supported by a couple of people who left Martin's department last year. Let us also assume that, after a somewhat difficult meeting with Martin (which you handled brilliantly) Martin recognizes that there is scope for improvement and he is anxious to work with you towards a solution. Let us also suppose that David and his colleagues want a successful resolution.

Study the worksheets and identify which factors, in your opinion, are worthy of attention in solving this particular problem. Below, we have summarized the scope of each worksheet.

Worksheet	Summary of the scope of the worksheet
☐ 1 *Our arena*	Awareness of the larger picture; the relationship between the manager's domain and the outside world.
☐ 2 *Our enterprise*	What are our unique characteristics? How does it all work?
☐ 3 *Business sense*	How well equipped is the manager to make good business decisions, based on customer needs, enterprise goals and so forth?
☐ 4 *Basic management responsibilities*	Stewardship of personnel (and other key resources).
☐ 5 *Developing the business*	Improvement in the use of resources.
☐ 6 *Planning*	Vision of the future and creating the means of getting there.
☐ 7 *Relationships*	Influence on the behaviour of others.

☐ 8 *Communication*	How good are lines of communication, in and out?
☐ 9 *Personal effectiveness*	Hands-on capabilities.
☐ 10 *Personnel development*	Measurement, sensitivity and skills at developing personnel.
☐ 11 *Motivation*	Employee satisfaction. What is it? How to manage it?
☐ 12 *Formal education and experience*	Properly equipped for the job?
☐ 13 *Some personality factors*	How to be a paragon among managers, assuming all the other factors are excellent!

Our 'solution' follows, but, of course, it is no more correct than yours is. It could not be, with such fragmentary knowledge of an imaginary set of situations and people.

Over to you

Using the management development worksheets; the case of the leapfrogged manager

■ *Planning*

Involve Martin's group in the planning process.

■ *Personal effectiveness*

Manage own time according to business priorities.

■ *Relations*

Establish a spirit of teamwork and team spirit within the group.

■ *Communication*

Create an environment for constructive criticism and new ideas.

Understand people by being a good observer and listener.

Explain the background and reason for decisions, guidance and so forth.

■ *Personnel development*

Be a good coach for the personnel.

■ *Motivation*

Create conditions for job satisfaction and high motivation.

Inspire people in defining job objectives.

Involve people in defining job objectives.

■ *Some personality factors*

Be honest (keep promises; make objective evaluations).

Be open-minded (have good self-knowledge; admit mistakes).

Give and deserve trust (create the conditions for open, honest, risk-free discussions; treat people fairly).

Be a role-model (demonstrate the important factors above).

If we had to select just one item for improvement, it would be under the heading 'planning'. If Martin involved his people in the planning process, *and did it well*, it would contribute to the improvement of a number of the other items we have chosen, such as:

- establish a spirit of teamwork
- create an environment for constructive criticism and new ideas
- understand people by being a good observer and listener

- explain the background for decisions and so forth.

Now we can look in our 'Management development tool-box' (see page 78) and see how Martin can be helped to do a good job of involving his people in the planning process. Some possibilities are:

- special job objectives aimed at a particular developmental aspect
- use of consultants when breaking new ground
- formal management education programmes
- you as a role model
- on-the-job training—receiving coaching from you.

This might be the right situation for the neutral outsider, the external consultant. Martin and his group would work together and learn together. There would be a visible commitment from you to follow through and reach a solution. There should be a quick and visible early success.

Then, you have to ensure continuity, perhaps by means of special job objectives for Martin and, of course, you as a role model. You must also keep a close watch on the personality factors.

On-the-job training (coaching from you) might be just as effective. In fact, this is such an important tool, it deserves its own section.

Coaching managers

When we interview managers about their development, they almost invariably answer by telling us about the latest management course they have attended or the one that was cancelled or postponed. The same people also agree that the most important development takes place on the job—learning by doing. Yet, the first response is to describe formal education courses. Why? We think it is a case of the on-the-job development being something that just 'happens to happen'. No conscious coaching activities take place and the middle manager concerned takes no initiatives in this respect. Here is an area with an enormous potential for improvement.

The problem is, how can you implement effective coaching in practice when you are so seldom present when your managers are performing their various tasks? Also, how do you do this effectively without conflicting with the earlier important advice, to keep out of the way.

Is the option to leave them alone to sink or swim, to learn by trial and error? Unfortunately, while there may be some quite intense learning going on as a result of error (failure?), such errors can be costly. In some enterprises they are not tolerated, despite a publicly declared 'policy' of encouraging the taking of risks.

> IBM even had this enshrined in a book written by Thomas J. Watson Jr., the son of the founder, *A Business And Its Beliefs*. It was first published by McGraw-Hill as long ago as 1963, but cultural attitudes take a very long time to change. It says, '... one point on which I have real concern. It has to do with the cautious attitude of so many young men in middle management today. They seem reluctant to stick their necks out or bet on a hunch. ... I wish we could stir them up a bit and encourage a little more recklessness among this group of decision makers. Every time we've moved ahead in IBM, it was because someone was willing to take a chance, put his head on the block, and try something new.'

Note the 'put his head on the block'! So you *know* what will happen if you fail. With this kind of statement from the boss, there is the danger that you develop a large number of risk-averse managers at all levels.

Errors are a powerful way of learning, but they are not efficient. If your monthly reviews are well done and your coaching, too, the errors should become visible before they strike. The learning can take place with limited damage, at most.

Good managers also keep their eyes open. Not only do they observe and learn the good things from mentors, they learn from *other* people's mistakes; a much less painful process.

Good coaching is also important (with other management development tools) because some situations may arise only once in a manager's career. This is not the time to fail—trial and error, sink or swim are to be avoided.

It is worth repeating here what we said about on-the-job coaching from you on page 79:

> Coaching by you is something which you and one of your managers have formally agreed on as being a development activity—you plan it together, you support the manager throughout the activity and you give appropriate feedback at the end.

The starting point is that both you and the manager agree on the need and you both try to find something in the manager's job to use for development, for personal coaching from you. Here are some suggestions.

- *Events* There are occasions when you may naturally be present when the manager is 'performing', inside or outside the enterprise. This may be running a meeting, kicking off a project, giving information, anything. You must avoid 'upstaging' the manager, however, if you are the senior manager present. Early on, you have to make it clear to all that yours is a subsidiary role in this affair. Be careful, too, to sustain this subsidiary role, by the way you position your chair, for example.
- *Dress rehearsals* At times, the manager can involve you in a dress rehearsal of some event. The manager describes the scenario of the coming event. You give constructive feedback. At the same time, you update your view of the manager, of course.
- *Delegation* Delegation is an effective method for coaching managers. The manager gets the opportunity to practise a new task, or role, and to broaden skills.

  Delegated tasks should have clearly defined limits. They start with a clear description of what to do and how to do it. The manager is your alter ego in this new role, perhaps representing you (and the enterprise) on some local government enquiry, for example. You should pay special attention to the positive and the negative aspects of the experience so that you *both* can learn.
- *Completed staff work* You must insist on it from your managers. This is an important element of coaching by you. Each case must be well prepared before being presented to you. Equally, this means that when you are presenting to your managers, perhaps in your management committee, or to one of your manager's groups, your presentation has to gleam with the polish of being really thoroughly well prepared.
- *Creating development tasks* If you are serious about improving the Total Quality of your managers, you will have to resolve the old dilemma between short- and long-term objectives. The 'business as usual' activities of your manager might be the ones having the biggest impact on short-term objectives today. However, if you have decided, in your wisdom as the senior manager, to make a special investment in a development task for one of your managers, and it is in conflict with normal operations today, *you have to stick to it.* Your job includes looking further ahead than your managers. Somehow, you must ensure that the manager has sufficient time and focus to do an excellent job of it, and you must follow up, support and track progress.
- *You as a role model* If you want your managers to improve in keeping their groups informed, you had better be sure you live up to whatever standard you set. Any deficiencies on your part will shine like beacons. There are some things

where you really *must* set an example, as a role model. Timeliness, an uncluttered working environment, no security violations, such as memoranda marked 'confidential' being left on your desk and (embarrassingly) collected by the security people during the night. These are basic things. Accept, however, that you cannot be exemplary in everything. There could be a variety of reasons for you not having the charisma of Tom Peters or Sir John Harvey-Jones when it comes to presentation techniques. You may not be a role model, but you can dig into your management development tool-box to find another way of improving your manager's presentation skills, or whatever.

These are six methods for coaching managers, either by direct involvement or by example. Please add others to this list, summarized below, that you may have experienced:

- events
- dress rehearsals
- delegation
- completed staff work
- creating development tasks
- you as a role model.

The case of the retrogressive manager

Brenda is the manager you rated most highly as a result of your work in Part 2, 'Acclimatizing to the new role', so it comes as a surprise and a disappointment when she comes to you and says, 'I don't really want to be a manager any more'.

Let's go back and look at your notes and impressions of Brenda up to now.

When you went through Check-list 3, 'Questions to your managers', with her, you were impressed by the manner and the content of her answers. Here is someone who is skilled at the job and is reliable. Order and organization prevail. There appears to be a good spirit in her group. She has excellent education plans for her people. She has had her group for a number of years, a clear indicator of the value of continuity. In summary, she comes across as a skilled, professional manager, able to use all the tools of her trade. She knows all the rules and regulations, the processes and systems. She has good relationships with all her people, is in touch with their daily activities and has an open, on-going dialogue with them about their long-term development.

Brenda gives you some clear indicators of areas for improvement regarding your *other* managers.

Based on these impressions, your initial rating of the factors bearing on the results of Brenda's group look like this:

- efficiency   B (good)
- effectiveness   B (good)
- employee satisfaction   B (good)
- ability to secure resources   B (good)
- ability to manage change   E (don't know).

You cautiously resisted the temptation to give her 'A' ratings in case you were dazzled by your first impressions. The 'E' rating for ability to manage change is natural enough. At that stage, you were not really in a position to know.

When you went through the 13 worksheets, you did it initially for the job itself, not with Brenda in mind as a person. This contrasts with the way you used the worksheets for Martin. In his case, you had a problem with the manager. In Brenda's case, there were no obvious problems. Your assessment of the key areas for *anyone* in her particular job to excel at was as follows:

- understand the objectives of the enterprise
- find information about the enterprise and share it with the group
- understand the need for change and communicate it
- explain the background for decisions and guidelines
- base proposals and decisions on a broad view of the enterprise
- take new initiatives to develop the group
- create a positive climate for ideas, be enthusiastic
- inspire the people in the group to work towards a shared vision.

Since then, you have had three monthly review meetings with Brenda and your other managers. You have 'dropped your thermometer case', so to speak, a few times and managed to glimpse beneath the surface.

Among Brenda's undoubted strengths are the excellence of her personnel plans, her ability to let key people move on to other departments and her ability to bring new people into her team. You then find that the turnover of personnel in her group is considerably higher than that of any other of your managers. Is this a good sign, however, or a bad one? Another note of some disquiet is the feeling that she has become somewhat transparent, passing information like a passive relay station without adding any real value in the process.

Nevertheless, you are very happy to have her on your management team. She is a good manager with the potential to be even better, and now she tells you she does not want to be *any* kind of manager!

When you ask her what has brought this about, you find that it has been a gradual process. She tells you she has felt as if she is running out of steam; that the pleasure and drive of the job are not there any more. There was no single event that caused this, it just developed over time to the point where she is now, realizing that the manager's job does not give her any satisfaction any more. (Note that now you must go back and change your own self-assessment score for management satisfaction to 'D' (bad). Remember the Martin and David situation? The same reasoning applies to you.)

'What am I doing all day?', she asks. 'Planning budgets, juggling and fiddling with numbers, pleading for an additional place on a fully-booked course, trying to find temps to fill our vacancies, making overtime statistics, running group meetings that half of them complain about because they take too much time. The other half complain because they don't feel properly informed. I want to get away from all this hassle and do something more exciting and rewarding, that's all!'

She tells you that she has not really felt that she has been a good manager recently, despite good results and external appearances. She believes her group deserves someone more enthusiastic. She wants to leave before she becomes a truly bad manager, saying 'My group does not deserve that'.

Things are not yet desperate. The change is not urgent as far as Brenda is concerned. (What about you? How do you feel about that 'D' you have just given yourself?) She commits to managing the group for as long as you want her to, but, in the long run (or should it be the short run?), knowing her feelings, she looks to you to find a solution.

The plateau problem

Brenda is on the edge of being 'plateaued' in her job. A vital aspect of your stewardship role is to recognize the symptoms of being plateaued, and know what to do about it.

Plateauing *usually* refers to the manager (or any other employee) who is valued by the enterprise, but for whom there are no prospects for promotion or advancement. This does not describe Brenda. There are other ways of becoming plateaued, however.

Dr Judith Bardwick of the University of California, San Diego, distinguishes between three different kinds of plateauing:

- structural
- content
- in life.

Structural plateauing is used to describe those people who realize that they are not going to be promoted any more. Almost everyone becomes structurally plateaued naturally, because the higher you go, the fewer places there are available, particularly in a hierarchical organization. Therefore, it is axiomatic that almost everyone will reach their highest job level long before they reach retirement age. Structural plateauing is endemic now because of pressures to 'delayer' organizations and release large numbers of middle managers. So, there are even fewer opportunities. We referred to this in Part 1, 'The changing middle management job'.

The problem is worse now than in the past because it is happening sooner, and it hurts. Whereas 20 years ago, structural plateauing might have happened to someone in their forties or fifties, when it might be tolerably acceptable, today it is being experienced by people in their thirties.

Plateauing is particularly galling for people in their thirties if they were recognized as being high-flyers at an early stage in their careers, with all the associated high expectations. For them, what is known as 'burnout' is a high possibility, characterized by extreme frustration, rage and exhaustion. Previously they were regarded as outstanding, the élite; now they are merely competent and ordinary. This can be quite devastating when the promotions stop. It is particularly a problem for those enterprises (and their people) that recruited only the brightest and most ambitious people. If the enterprise also has a high-flyer fast stream, the inherent dangers are bigger, because:

- those who are *not* on the fast stream know it, and they are disgruntled
- the vast majority of those *on* the fast stream will suffer devastation when the inevitable plateauing hits them.

Previously it used to be said that people will rise to the level of their own incompetence (the Peter Principle). Nowadays, many people are going to remain stuck *below* levels in which they *would* have been successful. You are going to have to create a new dream, so to speak, which emphasizes objectives that can be respected and achieved, but no longer include marked advances in terms of promotion, power and money.

Content plateauing relates to the need for challenge in the job. Most jobs can be mastered in three or four years. After that, many people become content plateaued. They may become passive. They may withdraw from people and work. Eventually, they can become thoroughly depressed, even clinically so.

Brenda is not there, yet, but she is showing some of the symptoms (passively passing on information, for example). The important thing is that she recognizes that she is in danger of becoming plateaued (she told you she wants to leave before she becomes a truly bad manager), even if she has never heard of the term. In most cases, you will not be told directly. You have to find out, to recognize the symptoms. Nearly all plateaued people who are really upset have never talked about their feelings with anyone.

Plateaued in life is much more serious than structural or content plateauing. These people feel that their entire life is repetitive. Every day and every week seems to be a long, predictable series of commitments to meet, and it is all the same as in the past—no change, no momentum—so there is no sense of the future. For these people, failure at work equals failure at *everything*.

The people most vulnerable to becoming plateaued in life are those whose commitment to work used to be total. Work became the only place in which achievements felt really important and were recognized. Work was where they gained a feeling of self-esteem and the vivid sense of being alive. Work was life and life was work. 'Burned out' people are in danger of being plateaued in life. They may feel that nobody in the enterprise, nor their family, knows or cares about the sacrifices they have made. They can feel utterly alone, rejected and desperate.

If you do nothing about Brenda's situation, she could eventually enter the unhappy content plateaued phase, then drift into the more morbid plateaued in life feeling. So, despite what she says about managing the group for as long as you want her to, you have to do something soon.

Unfortunately, we are stuck with a set of values that relate success and failure to positions in the management hierarchy. These expectations of a long and orderly management ladder are quite recent. The driving force that created them was the exceptional economic expansion between 1950 and 1975. The nineteenth-century organization illustrated in Part 1, 'The changing middle management job', prevailed, in fact, until the start of that boom, in many enterprises. There was nowhere really to go, so there were no plateau problems.

Maurice Hardaker worked during the 1960s for what was, at that time, the biggest firm of consulting engineers in the world, Merz and McLellan. It still had the same structure as when Charles Merz founded it at the turn of the century.

At the top were the partners, about a dozen of them. They owned the entire thing, personally. They sat at an Olympian height above everyone else. There were no managers, as such, just chief engineers of the various disciplines—mechanical, civil, electrical, transmission and so forth. Then there were the professional engineers. There was a bigger gap between a chief engineer and the partners than between that chief engineer and the tea lady. It was the difference between the payers and the paid. The team spirit and level of cooperation among the hundreds of professional engineers—the paid—were tremendous. Plateauing was an unknown, alien concept to the people working there.

Most organizations are not like this now, so plateauing is inevitable at all levels. In fact, many people at senior levels are plateaued *and* happy about it ('As well they might be!', say more junior colleagues), *but they dare not admit their contentedness* in case of repercussions. A change in the relentless 'onwards and upwards' drive could well produce a collective sigh of relief in the upper layers of the enterprise. However, these top managers do not see the daily stresses of office and factory life, they do not normally observe the revealing symptoms of being plateaued in a *negative* sense. Middle managers *should* see these things. This is why it is an important part of your stewardship role, specifically in relation to the total quality of your managers.

Notice that many people become plateaued in a positive sense, by the way. For these happy people, who are plateaued *and* satisfied with their work situation, who are content with their responsibilities and the mastery of their work, *leave them alone.* You have to reward them accordingly, of course, but your attention has to be focused on those of your managers who may become plateaued in a *negative* sense. They may feel like failures, causing them to lose interest because they are bored or angry. Their involvement with work becomes distant and it begins to show in their results. It is then that it also becomes a problem for the enterprise. Maintaining the plateaued manager's sense of purpose for the future is essential for the enterprise's health. This means that it is your concern. You have to know how to anticipate when negative plateauing is imminent, then deal with it effectively, in advance, if you are to improve and maintain the total quality of management.

Because the vast majority of people in any enterprise will inevitably become plateaued, it is essential that they feel good about themselves and their work, despite being plateaued. They are the backbone of the enterprise, after all.

Stars get a lot of attention. People in trouble also tend to receive a lot of attention, especially if they interfere with the general production of results. The others, however—the majority who are competent, experienced and dependable—tend to receive very little. You have to keep your eyes on that 80 per cent who may drift unseen into the negative aspects of being plateaued. This is completely the opposite of the usual 80/20 rule, where 20 per cent of the resource (inventory, for example) needs close attention. Here, you have to worry about that big 80 per cent.

CHECK-LIST 8 Symptoms of plateauing

Study this list carefully and ask yourself whether any of your own managers persistently show one or more of these symptoms, or a trend to an increase in them (then consider yourself, by the way). This list is not arranged in any particular order.

Over to you

Plateau symptom	Manager 1	Manager 2	Manager 3	Manager 4	Manager 5
Boredom					
Absenteeism					
Argumentativeness					
Depression					
Rage					
Anxiety					
Irritability					
Impatience					
Drug use					
Excessive eating					
Excessive drinking					
Excessive smoking					
Low morale					
Cynicism					
Dependence					
Conformity					
Withdrawal					
Passivity					
A growing tiredness/ conservatism/staleness					

- Watch out for workaholics. They increase the time that they work, but they do not work well. They just work longer for the same result. Then they become depressed; a depression that increases over time.
- Watch out for signs of defence and maintenance of the status quo.
- Watch out for a greater emphasis on the ritualistic aspects of work. ('Where's my form?! Nothing moves until I get my form!') Watch out for the emerging bureaucrat who ruthlessly pursues the unimportant at the expense of the real value-adding work.
- Watch out for over-elaboration of procedures, activities and status symbols, the unnecessary complexity and over-fussy methods introduced to maintain an artificially high level of activity, and, thereby, justification to oneself and to others (and think of the impact on costs and cycle times for the enterprise).
- Watch out for symptoms of stress in the way people may try to manage *themselves* in the situation of being plateaued—obsessive involvement in physical activities, love affairs, health and diet concerns, pop psychology movements and so forth.

Managing through the plateau problem

The climate of trust that you must create is important for you to be able to see and diagnose the symptoms of plateauing. It is *essential* for you to effect a cure.

In a nutshell, you have to maintain or regenerate interest and motivation in people who, for realistic and appropriate reasons, are no longer involved, creative or productive in their work. Better yet, you should anticipate and prevent the problems of plateauing. You cannot prevent it actually happening, though.

It is easy to feel helpless when there are no more promotion slots available, nor money for salary increases. This is because the typical manager's view has been: reward = promotion + money. If managers consider these to be the only *meaningful* rewards, and they have not got them to give, they are liable to give nothing. However, *anything* can be a reward if it is valued by the recipient, particularly if there is an additional sense of achievement because others may be competing for it.

Some enterprises are changing their reward systems by linking them with *results* (remember that word?). The reward is for what you *produce* rather than *where you sit*. Thus, a manager can be recognized for what is actually done, rather than as a nascent (but statistically unlikely) CEO. Such enterprises have to produce management education and training that helps their managers to do their work, rather than presenting them with idealized models of managing—which heaven preserve us from doing in this book!

We can learn something about attitudes to rewards from people who are plateaued from the start, and they know it. Employees in retail shops, hotels and restaurants at the operative level tend to be a mobile population (at great cost and inconvenience to their employers), and they know they are not going to rise very far, if at all, with their current employer. It would be easy to suppose that money would be the overriding determinant of loyalty, but this thinking is wrong.

The Marriott Corporation found that only about 20 per cent of workers in its Roy Rogers fast food restaurants (since sold) and 30 per cent of its hotel workers regarded pay as their primary reason for working there. When 13 000 workers in retail shops in the United States were asked to list in order the 18 reasons for working there, they ranked 'good pay' third. In first place was 'appreciation for work done', with 'respect for me as a person', second.

When similar employees were asked how their company could be improved, to create a better place to work, employees replied that they wanted better training, better communications with their supervisors and, above all, they wanted their bosses, 'to make me feel like I make a difference'.

The important thing here is that these people *knew* they were plateaued (even if they had never heard of the term) by the nature of the job. Already you should be able to see the importance of things other than rank and money. The key is that your people (and you) have to *know* that they are all very likely to be plateaued. You have to be honest. You have to be forthright about how you perceive prospects for each of your managers. People want negative feedback as well as positive, *and it is a lot easier when you have that climate of trust* (people who are already plateaued may resent a lot of positive feedback, finding it dishonest and patronizing). Regular appraisal and counselling reviews (or performance appraisal) have to be totally honest and realistic, rather than taking the easy escape into a column of 'B' ratings and some platitudes.

Remember, those who have plateaued have to get beyond their bitterness and their fantasy that, if only they had been allowed to realize their ambitions, life would be marvellous. They must somehow revalue aspects of work so that it can be satisfying, or fun—why not? New commitments must be made to enable them to feel that they are productive and making contributions *they* can respect. Those who can go beyond the frustrated ambitions of their youth can have a great time in what used to be called middle age—and it can really *feel* like middle age if you become plateaued in your early thirties—but it can also become one of the fullest and most creative phases of life. Such people become more honest with themselves. The result is they can be more responsive to people. They no longer need to have power or dominate others to get things done and produce good, satisfying results. You are not being brutal or kidding anyone by being honest and forthright; just realistic.

For some people, the plateau problems can be resolved by changes in work. Others may require interventions that include but go beyond work and may involve family members. Here we are focusing only on the work-related opportunities.

When the nature and the (almost) inevitability of plateauing are recognized and accepted, you can then go on to review alternative motivation and reward mechanisms. None of this should get in the way of your managers who *will* make it to the top, by the way. Indeed, it should increase their potential value and make that value more visible to a wider community.

Check-list 9 lists possible approaches to managing through the real problems of plateauing.

CHECK-LIST 9   Approaches to the plateau problem

☐ *Appraisal and counselling* (You may use a different form of words, such as 'performance reviews', for example.) If this is done honestly and well, people gain a clear knowledge of where they stand. The negative aspects of plateauing will be reduced if people see that there is a close match between your judgements, as expressed in the appraisal and counselling, and their modified expectations. The 'easy way out' approach to appraisal and counselling can lead to exactly the opposite effect. We are back again to the need for you to be consistent, fair and to have clear communications.

A well done appraisal and counselling lets your managers know you are really considering possible future placements for them. It is valuable because it lets your managers know what they do well and what needs improving. You must *help* them to improve, of course, by using some of the techniques described here and elsewhere.

A badly done appraisal and counselling is like the Persian Messenger Syndrome in reverse. Your managers receive only good news because you are uncomfortable or evasive about criticizing them and about their future prospects. They can then interpret the outcome as an endorsement of their own (too high) expectations of advancement if they continue to perform so 'well'.

☐ *Education and training* There is an important difference between these. If someone has a teenage daughter who comes home from school one day and announces, 'Today we had sex education', there will not normally be much concern. Training, though, would be another matter!

Your managers will need both education *and* training. Some of this will be the normal sort of thing required for effective performance of the job and for management development. Some may be specifically targeted to avoid or assuage the effects of plateauing. Some may be needed to prepare them to make a full and enthusiastic contribution to some of the other suggested approaches that follow.

☐ *Increase the scope and status of the present job* Excellence then becomes recognized by the professional community as a whole. This is how you keep good salespeople selling, good researchers doing research. We have all seen such people promoted to administrative jobs because it was the only way up. They often do not do that job very well, and often they are miserable about it. The enterprise loses their valuable talents for producing results that matter.

> Scientists in the United Kingdom's Civil Service are recognized by 'individual merit' distinction that enhances both reputation and salary without having to divert them from doing excellent science. A similar merit recognition system operates for doctors in the UK's National Health Service.

The same approach can be applied to non-specialist managers. The job has to emphasize self-esteem, self-development and self-motivation.

☐ *Lateral transfers* Consider lateral transfers that involve different responsibilities and corresponding changes in the job content. This can help content plateauing, but not structural plateauing.

☐ *Short-term special assignments* These can be beneficial, but *only if* there is a corresponding relief from some regular duties.

☐ *Short-term project teams* These allow people to take on more responsibility in a more mixed environment, and can deliver surprisingly good results. Peoples' jobs, and the challenge of the jobs, can be broadened without them being promoted. They begin to see the almost infinite possibilities of working together as a team, compared with the very finite limits of an individual.

☐ Here is a list of other possible options, all of which can add dignity and worth to the individual's life and work:

- *mentors*, perhaps within a broader scope of the enterprise
- *internal consultants*
- *community leaders*
- *visiting lecturers* or *speakers*
- *liaison* with government and other bodies.

☐ *Reorganization into autonomous business units* This can help considerably. Though this may be beyond the scope of your present job, you can be involved in 'selling the religion' to top management. Senior managers effectively become CEOs when they head these autonomous units. This gives them and their management team the challenge of developing a new business one that has to deliver results, without anyone being formally promoted.

☐ *Ceremonies and symbols of all kinds* These can make the recipient feel recognized and valued, even in very large organizations. They should not just be handed out, however; they have to be earned. Also, they should be awarded in a manner that lets the individual's value be seen by as large a community as possible. Internal newspapers are a powerful means of doing this and, of course, there are the more ceremonial occasions. The options available are limited only by your own imagination. For example, awarding a dinner for two to a manager who has done an excellent piece of work need not cost a fortune, but the effect on a manager and partner can be very positive.

☐ *Let your managers read this book* This section, at least, should make them aware of the facts of life with regard to plateauing, and prepare them for the day when a manager *does* get promoted to replace you or someone else. More important, everything here applies also to your managers in *their* jobs. They *also* have to watch out for symptoms of plateauing and (perhaps with your help) do something about it for the sake of the individual and the enterprise.

The most hopeful view of the future is that the new organization structures that we described in Part 1, 'The changing middle management job', will of themselves reduce the incidence of negative plateauing. Delayering distributes greater responsibility among people within fewer hierarchical levels. A shift from hierarchy to cross-functional process management provides a much richer environment in which to participate. Either approach requires a much heavier emphasis on teamwork and project work, more empowerment, a broader scope of involvement inside and beyond the boundary of the enterprise. It should be rewarding, and fun!

Motivation of managers

The various approaches to resolving the problems of plateauing described in Check-list 9, 'Approaches to the plateau problem', can all be viewed as means for motivating your managers. However, for plateauing, the objective is to effect a cure. Motivation is more preventive in nature. In this section we shall look at motivation in the more general sense. Motivation of your managers should be high, of course, because it features as a key factor in *your own* self-assessment of:

- efficiency
- effectiveness

- *management satisfaction*
- ability to secure resources
- ability to manage change.

You have to give yourself a 'D' until you solve Brenda's problem. But what happens afterwards? What is the satisfaction level of the rest of your managers, those who are not yet plateaued, or even approaching this state?

We can learn something from the people in the TQM field. They have the concept the 'cost of quality'. It concerns the different cost elements of simply getting things right, resulting in the following formula:

cost of quality = prevention cost + appraisal cost + fixing cost

The fixing cost is much higher than either of the other two. Consider the example of the necessary design change to equipment installed in customers' premises, necessary for safety reasons, that we discussed earlier. It was an imaginary example. Here are some real ones.

In February 1990, all supplies of Perrier water were recalled, *world-wide*.

In 1959, Ford launched the Edsel car. It had many innovations, but terrible quality problems. The estimated loss per car was $1117, a total of about $250 million in 1959 money.

More recently, General Motors had to recall 1836 of its Saturn cars. It gave the owners new ones, an unprecedented response in this industry.

The Japanese do it, too. In December 1989, the Lexus division of Toyota had to recall *all* its LS 400 cars because of three separate defects.

Tricity Bendix had to advertise to owners of all of their MT520 and MV510 microwave ovens sold in 1992 to, '... stop using the product immediately and remove the plug from the socket'.

Other recent advertising about *faulty* products (this must be the worst possible form of advertising) have come from Thermos, Braun, Halfords and Van Smirren Seafoods, for example. You can probably make your own list.

The fixing costs to the companies concerned is colossal, and these are just the big ones that make it into the media.

Excellent appraisal is necessary to prevent these products getting out, and it costs a fraction of the fixing costs. There still remains a cost, however. Bad-quality products that are trapped before they get out still have to be fixed (or scrapped), but this costs much less than if they had escaped and then had to be fixed. This cost of quality concept is not confined to the commercial sector. It was discovered in 1993 that large numbers of patients had received the wrong level of radiation therapy in part of the UK National Health Service. For some patients, sadly, it was too late to 'fix it'.

Investment in prevention is one of the main messages of TQM. Despite an initial cost, the total cost of quality is dramatically reduced when the focus shifts to prevention cost. Do it well, and the appraisal cost reduces, too.

> About 40 years ago, the then Chairman of Rolls-Royce was interviewed by a writer who was preparing a book on the motor car industry. The Chairman was asked how the company reacted when a 'lemon', a bad car, escaped. 'It must happen sometimes, even to Rolls-Royce', said the interviewer. The Chairman replied that it was completely impossible. When asked how he could be so certain, he replied, 'The man at the gate would not let it out'.

Total Quality is everyone's responsibility. Let's go back to your specific responsibility for the Total Quality of management.

Because you are dealing with human beings, there is not only the financial cost to the enterprise of prevention, appraisal and fixing, there is the emotional cost for the person concerned. Also, the financial and emotional costs are much higher for fixing than for prevention. This is why your investments in motivation for your managers are worthwhile, as just one form of prevention.

The basic rules of motivation that you learned as a first-line manager apply to managers as much as they do to other employees. It is easy for non-managers (and some managers) to believe that when someone is made a manager, they slip into some sort of cadre, fully formed and all rather similar. But each one has the same human needs for motivation at work as anyone else. The office, the piece of carpet, the car and the corporate credit card give a boost, all right, but it is a relatively short-term one, and managers are all different. They have different reasons for becoming managers in the first place. Find out why and you will see something of their differing motivation needs.

Managers are only human

Managers (and this includes you) have one thing in common with everyone else in the enterprise: they are human beings. They are also all different. They are subject to the same, complicated set of things that motivate everyone else. Understand what they are for each of your managers and you will understand how to motivate them.

For an excellent description of these basic human drivers, see *Managing People At*

Work by John Hunt, who is the Plowden Professor of Organization Behaviour at the London Business School (McGraw-Hill, 1992). He has developed a set of questions which, when answered, provide a remarkably accurate picture of what drives any particular individual. The picture may change with time and circumstances, but the underlying pattern remains quite constant for any individual adult.

John Hunt has studied the responses of many thousands of managers in 'Western' cultures and has identified eight different goals that we all try to satisfy at work, and each of us has a different combination of them. For any individual, some are normally stronger than others (his book also reveals interesting national and cultural differences in this). The following is a brief summary of the motivations given in his book.

- *Comfort goals* These are the goals of a comfortable life-style. While money is an important element, it tends not to be the dominant motivator, except for a very small number of people. This goal has the largest variability—it is less likely to be a dominant goal for a top manager than for a clerical or process worker, for example.

- *Structure goals* These are linked to comfort goals, but rather than relating to a comfortable life-style, they relate to the search for a definition of what is required of each individual. People for whom this is the dominant goal will probably be much less comfortable in the looser, less structured organizations to which we referred earlier.

- *Relationship goals* Some people need to form strong interpersonal relationships. Others are loners. Beware of the loner manager designing jobs for people who are motivated by relationships.

- *Recognition and status goals* Recognition is one of the strongest goals among high achievers. People for whom this is the dominant goal can never get enough of it. Managers have virtually unlimited opportunities for rewarding such individuals.

- *Power goals* This has the highest average score as a motivator among 5500 European managers. Their primary goal is the opportunity to influence, control and reward the behaviour of subordinates. So, it probably describes you and your managers. Yet, direct managerial power is decreasing, as we have described. You will have to exercise your power more by influencing. And you must find innovative means of rewarding, other than by money and promotion. Hence the need to understand the fundamental goals of your managers.

- *Autonomy, creativity and growth goals* This manifests itself in a search for independence, for opportunities to be original and creative, for growth and challenge. Such people may be difficult to manage, but they are responsible for new businesses, techniques, products, services, innovative approaches to all kinds of things. They tend not to be good managers, in the traditional sense, and a traditional enterprise can accommodate only a limited number of them. However, they may be just the sort of people needed in the newer, more open and flexible organizations, or in high technology-based start-up enterprises.

Motivation of managers is as vital as motivation of employees. Can you imagine a demotivated manager creating a highly motivated set of employees—a key factor in achieving results? A more likely result is a negative influence, which your enterprise cannot afford.

Let's look at some more of your managers.

Alex was made a manager quite early in his career, though if you asked him he would say that the promotion was not a day too early! He says he always wanted to be a manager, and he certainly worked hard at it. What is he looking for? What is the attraction of the job for Alex?

Alex would probably say that he wanted to make a career, to earn his spurs and become a top manager, and you do not get to be a top manager without starting as a first-line manager. So, the sooner you start, the better. Other people might say he is driven by the desire to have power. Others, like you, who know him better, would use words like 'ambition', or 'having responsibility and challenge' as being his primary motivators, with 'challenge' probably being the most dominant. Alex clearly likes to pit himself against new situations in which there are problems and uncertainty. He is prepared to take risks, so he is not one of those grey, risk-averse corporate time-servers, by any means. But he is not an opportunist either. He has added value wherever he has worked. He never leaves a piece of work half done and he certainly has not chosen the easy jobs. Alex has the willpower and determination to keep pushing until he reaches his goal.

Yet, he is also a good people manager. He does not seem to have natural leadership qualities, but he so much wants to succeed, he has worked hard at these aspects of his work and has emerged as a very professional manager in regard to his people, too.

What makes him keep going? What gives him the 'buzz' that maintains his momentum and enthusiasm for the job? Success. Alex sees success as the reward. He just does not accept failure as an option. And being successful gives Alex a chance to shine. He is often asked to speak on courses and to meet external visitors, and he loves it. He would probably have a high score under 'recognition and status'.

So, to keep Alex's motivation and satisfaction high, you have to provide him with:

- opportunities to shine
- opportunities to be successful, both in his own estimation and his results for the enterprise
- opportunities to move on to new challenges.

Consider Check-list 6, 'A management development tool-box', and Check-list 9, 'Approaches to the plateau problem'. Together they provide a rich and varied menu from which to choose the right sequence of events for Alex. But you must also ensure that he is fully informed about plateauing. It could hit someone like Alex very hard, whether at his present level, or later, when he may be at your level, or higher.

Betty, on the other hand, actively avoided being made a manager for some years. She had a distinguished specialist career, yet she also exhibited the right qualities to be a manager. Eventually, one day she must have persuaded herself it was time to try something new, having the confidence that she could probably do the management job as well as most other people. Betty is an example of the specialist who did become a good manager, but it was *she* who decided when the time was right.

She is so different to Alex, yet both are good managers. Where Alex looks for challenge, Betty sees a set of difficult tasks that must be skilfully handled. Alex achieves results by managing his energy well, while Betty uses a cool mind and a warm heart. (This is not sexist, by the way—we have all seen successful women who are like Alex in approach and successful men who are like Betty in approach. Vive la différence!) However, like Alex, she wants recognition for a job well done, and why not? She wants to feel this recognition from those closest to her at work, but also from her peers, her family and from managers above her.

The big difference between Betty and Alex is her dependence on honesty and fairness from those with whom she is dealing. Things like broken promises, failed commitments, dirty tricks and so forth make Alex fight. These just make Betty sad. Her goal profile would probably show a much higher score against 'relationship goals' than would Alex's.

Probable motivation factors for Betty would include:

- an honest and fair working environment
- recognition from others
- her own self-esteem
- a feeling of being an important contributor to the enterprise.

Carl was more or less coerced into being a manager about ten years ago, and he is still there. He was the most experienced person around when the requirement arose, so his manager persuaded him.

He took on the new role for a number of reasons. First, it was quite difficult to turn down such a flattering and potentially rewarding proposal. Apart from anything else, to refuse would have been tantamount to an admission that he was not yet ready to take on the responsibility. Second, he trusted his manager and thought, 'If he believes I'll make a good manager, then I'll probably be all right. He'll give me the help and support I'll need'. Third, it could be viewed as disloyal to the enterprise, the way it was put to him.

Sadly, neither Carl nor his manager really did reflect on what it takes to be a good manager. There was an empty box on the organization chart and putting Carl's name in it meant that his manager could turn to other problems.

Carl went on a course for new managers and learned about legislation and regulations, motivation theories and the golden rules of delegation. Then he came back and spent the next ten years being an administrator, rather than a manager in the sense of Brenda, Betty and Alex. These last three actively moved the enterprise forwards, using their different styles.

This was all right when Carl was first promoted, but now he is getting a bit of a reputation as being an obstacle rather than a contributor to progress. The root cause was his manager appointing the wrong person for all the wrong reasons, then neglecting Carl's subsequent development as a manager.

What motivates Carl? He would probably have a high score in 'comfort'. Do you *need* to motivate him? Is he permanently but happily plateaued, administering his little empire, adequately enough—there are no disasters—but not really innovating in any way? If his little empire is off the main stream of the value-adding processes of the enterprise, but essential nevertheless as a lubricant or support for the core processes, *leave him alone* if he is happily plateaued. He doesn't need motivating. Just keep telling him what a good job he is doing, as long as it *is* good. Keep an eye on his results, as measured by:

- efficiency
- effectiveness
- employee satisfaction (watch this one, particularly)
- ability to secure resources
- ability to manage change (watch this one, too).

Also, watch out for any signs that he *is* being an obstacle.

On the other hand, if he is working in part of a linked set of business processes that are necessary to determine new product requirements, for example, or a process chain that designs, acquires (or makes) then distributes products or services to customers, you have a problem. These are not positions for a mere administrator. They are fine for Betty and Alex in their different ways, and for Brenda, too, before she got fed up with the hassle, but not for Carl. You have to motivate him *out* of the job, then put somebody there who *will* innovate to improve products or services, drive cost out of the enterprise, increase market share, quality, reduce cycle times and so forth.

Not easy. Taking him back to a professional job may be an answer, but after ten years as a manager, and an administrative style of manager at that, he might find re-entry rather difficult.

Now, what are you going to do about Brenda? She is a good manager and you do not want to lose her as a manager. She says she no longer wants the negative aspects of being a manager. What are the criteria of a good solution in her case?

Here is a suggestion.

1   Brenda is still a manager, probably with another group
2   she is happy and very motivated once more with her new group
3   you have secured a good new manager for her present group.

Despite her expressed wish *not* to continue as a manager, your first criterion is that she continues in this role. You do not want the enterprise to lose her excellent management qualities. Moreover, when good managers like Brenda leave this role, it can send the wrong kind of signals to other people. This can adversely affect your other efforts at improvement and your ability to recruit the best management potential.

Look through Check-list 9, 'Approaches to the plateau problem'. The fourth approach looks promising: 'Consider lateral transfers that involve different responsibilities and corresponding changes in job content. This can help content plateauing, but not structural plateauing'.

The challenge for you is to find the right *kind* of lateral transfer, one that will satisfy Brenda's probable motivation factors. First, you have to find out what these are (see John Hunt's book, *Managing People at Work*, McGraw-Hill, 1992 for example), then you must find the right place for her to experience them. Next, you must sell the idea to her (hopefully) new manager, and with her record this should not be too difficult. Then you have to sell the idea to Brenda. This might be *very* difficult.

Look at the second criterion for success: 'She is happy and very motivated once more with her new group'. When you know her motivation factors, this will help you in your search for the right job. If it *is* the right job, and you do a good job of selling it to Brenda, she will see the new challenges and opportunities to expand. Maybe the negative aspects of management will become a secondary issue then, from her perspective, though they will not go away, of course.

The third criterion is that you have a good new manager for Brenda's old group. With luck, you might be able to do a deal with her prospective new manager and get a bright, enthusiastic person from Brenda's new group to take over her old group when she leaves. We shall be discussing acquisition of the management resource later.

Either way, you have a lot of work to do to resolve Brenda's situation. It will not go away of its own accord. Soon, it will begin to show in the results of her group. Also, be prepared for her to stick to her guns and not want to continue to be a manager in any circumstances.

The other key factors

Up to now, we have concentrated mainly on the all-important 'softer' aspect of your stewardship role, the management satisfaction factor that impacts the Total Quality of your results. Here, we shall consider the 'harder' aspects of efficiency, effectiveness, ability to secure resources and the ability to manage change. We shall consider these aspects from your perspective, that is, you as a senior manager who has to deliver good results from your domain. You depend on your managers to do this, but, remember, their results are your results.

We shall take a business process approach. This can apply whether your enterprise is hierarchial, functional, process-orientated or whatever.

Regardless of the formal organization structure, people *do* things. They perform activities in business processes, sub-processes, tasks, call them what you will. And what they do is either customer-visible or it is not. So, the process approach is equally applicable whether you are in a research and development, finance, legal or marketing department; manufacturing, the Police, the Civil Service or whatever. Your managers and their people either do something useful or not. If it is something that does not add value in some way, they should stop. Your enterprise cannot afford the luxury of a cost without a corresponding benefit. Intangible benefits are not worth the intangible paper they can't be written on.

We recognize that it is sometimes difficult to define exactly what the value added for any given activity is, but it must be done. Here is one way.

Find out who are the 'customers' of the activity or process. Who cares whether it is done or not? They may be entirely internal; other people doing other activities who are employed within the same enterprise. Some 'customers' are external, however. These may be *real* customers, who pay you money in exchange for products and services (and who have the option of giving their money to your competitors). In this case, we are talking about a customer-visible process or activity. Other kinds of external 'customers' of the process may be advertising agencies, government agencies, your bankers and so forth. External suppliers of components and raw materials, for example, may also be external 'customers' of a *process* if it is one that delivers manufacturing schedules for suppliers to deliver in a Just-In-Time environment.

When you know that a process or activity has 'customers,' then you know that it has a reason to exist. We can assume that the 'customers' receive something from the particular process, something that they want or need to perform their own activities. Your bankers need accurate daily cash flow information if they are to exploit the short- and long-term investment opportunities, for example.

We also recognize that some people reject the entire notion that they have customers of any sort.

We found a group from the Legal Department of a large corporation to be quite vehement in their rejection of the idea that they had customers. Perhaps it is not sufficiently dignified for lawyers to have mere customers? We got around it (eventually) by getting them to accept the concept of 'users of their outputs', such as top management getting a view on the legal consequences of an action, advice on whether or not to sue, marketing people enquiring as to whether or not a particular approach would expose the corporation to legal problems in some way, and so forth.

This, though, is just semantics. The question is: who cares whether or not this particular individual goes to work? Who cares that the particular activity is performed, and is performed well? Who needs something for the performance of *their* activities that originates in *this* one?

If you cannot find anyone, then stop doing it. If in doubt, stop doing it anyway, then see if anyone notices.

Efficiency: cost performance

Every manager in every enterprise *should* know the answers to the following questions; now, today. The extent to which they do not know the answers is a measure of lack of control and the loss of a potential opportunity to drive cost out of the enterprise.

Your managers will not have been asked all of the questions before. Ask them now. It will take some time to get a complete set of answers (set a time limit), but they will be very revealing answers. Then, you can jointly plan how to exploit the opportunities revealed—jointly with individual managers and jointly with your entire management team, perhaps, for the really big opportunities.

CHECK-LIST 10   Efficiency: Cost performance

1 How many iterations are needed to produce the process output—the trial balance, the invoice, the advertising copy, the income tax assessment?

How does this compare with competitors?

How does this compare with the best-of-breed?

If you don't know, find out. You may learn something.

2 What are the biggest cost items in the process?

- Inter-enterprise (cross-charging and so forth, sometimes called 'Monopoly money')?
- External (real money that leaves the enterprise)?

3 What is the most rapidly growing cost element in the process?

4 What opportunities are there for others to do some of the process activities?

- Internal suppliers (A small amount of extra processing by an internal supplier of information to the billing process might make that process much faster, and with fewer iterations)

- External suppliers (Ford's suppliers send information on quality daily, on-line to Ford, which reduces Ford's costs of inspection and contributes to higher end-product quality)

- Internal customers (Perhaps you are delivering more than you need to. Perhaps your internal customer would prefer a smaller amount of really pure input—information, for example—to process in a more effective manner, rather than the huge printouts you have been sending for years)

- External customers (If they can do some of the work, and they are happy to do it, your costs go down and customer satisfaction goes up—remember McKesson, the pharmaceutical wholesaler that enabled its pharmacist customers to place purchase orders directly using hand-held terminals; the customers are doing the order entry work formerly done by McKesson personnel)

5 What is the cost of quality in the process? (cost of quality = prevention + appraisal + fixing cost, where fixing cost means the cost of fixing *after* the output has left the process, either to an internal customer—the trial balance, say—or to an external customer who receives a product with defects)

Now that you know them, how do the cost of quality elements compare with the best-of-breed?

6 How long is the 'rest' time between receipt of inputs and their use by the process? (People normally think of this in terms of inventories of components, raw materials or products in a retail outlet, for example, where just having them in stock (the 'float') costs money. The same applies to any other resource. What is the *information* 'float' in the process for example? Not only does it cost the process to have it there, it could cost your internal supplier much more to get that information to the process by the first of the month, say, than by the fifteenth, when it is actually used)

7 Economies of scale. What opportunities are there to reduce unit costs as volumes grow, or prevent them from increasing?

8 Learning curve. What economies can be made by increasing knowledge of the process by means of:

- technology
- skills
- procedures
- relationships?

Effectiveness: doing the right things

This is where the focus shifts to the customers of the process, the users of its outputs. Now that you know who the customers are—all of them—you can find out whether or not the outputs are what they really want. You only have to ask.

We start with the *real*, revenue-producing external customers; *they are the most important*. If in doubt, read again the definition of Total Quality/Competitiveness/Effectiveness (see page). They pay your salary.

CHECK-LIST 11   Effectiveness: doing the right things

1 How many defects are reported each month, say, by your external customers?

If you do not have the means to monitor defects in this way, how can you be sure you are doing a good job?

What is the trend regarding defects? Increasing? Decreasing? In either case, what caused the increase or decrease?

2 What is your external customer's perception of the quality of the process?

Has it increased or decreased in the last six months? If so, what caused the increase or decrease?

3 What is the mechanism by which customers may complain about process defects? How is the complaint handled, stored, analysed or distributed to concerned parties within and beyond the enterprise?

General Electric spends over $8 million a year on an on-line service to handle customer complaints. They make a profit out of it through increased customer loyalty, reduced warranty costs and increased sales—many people use the free telephone number to ask for product information. They make this profit because the process is extremely well done, staffed by extremely well-trained personnel, who have excellent technology at their fingertips. Also, General Electric learns an enormous amount each day about customers and their perceptions.

4 What is your customer's perception of the quality of your *competitor's* process? Do you know?

5 How do *lost* customers view the process, in comparison with that of their current supplier— your competitor?

6 What are the external customer's main value-adding activities?

What contribution does your process make?

Does your customer know the contribution made by your process?

How could you increase this contribution?

7 What opportunities are there to absorb some of your customers' activities/tasks into *your* process. (This may increase your costs, but it should strengthen the relationship between you and your customer's enterprises.) Examples might include:

- education and training
- data entry
- quality management
- design

Du Pont offers its customers a variety of information services, including electronic mail, quality data, computer-aided design and engineering, order status, materials specifications and business management tools.

8 How can you increase your customer's perception of the service content of your process?

For internal customers—and external 'customers' of a process who are not real, revenue-producing customers—most of the above questions remain relevant. Here are a few more that are not so orientated to *real* customers.

9 Which of your internal customers perform work in activities or processes that *are* customer-visible?

What is the impact of *your* process on the level of customer satisfaction with your *internal* customer's process? How can you improve it?

10 How often do you review/negotiate the needs of your internal customers:

- every three months
- every six months
- yearly
- never
- only when the shouting starts?

11 How many defects are reported each month, say, by:

- internal customers
- internal suppliers
- external suppliers?

Your bankers are external suppliers, so, if you give them poor-quality financial information, they cannot do the best job for you; if you are a manufacturer using Just-In-Time methods, your suppliers can only deliver correctly if your requirements are correct and in time for them.

The ability to secure resources

Your managers cannot begin to negotiate for their resources until they know what they need. They cannot know what they need until they know what they are supposed to do.

This takes us back once more to the need for you to have *clear communications*. It is essential for you to give unambiguous statements to each of your managers about what are their goals, aims objectives or whatever. In simpler terms, describe the *results* you want from each manager's domain. Then, each manager should be able to identify which resources are required to produce the needed results.

There are some fairly obvious resources, what we shall call *working* resources. They can be viewed as resources that stay within the manager's domain on a fairly long-term basis. Depending on the nature of the job, and the needed results, they may include:

- personnel
- plant and equipment
- a budget
- premises
- skills
- heat, light and power
- rules, regulations, standards

- systems and procedures
- files of current information
- archival information
- technology and so forth.

Quite often, they come with the job. They are inherited from the previous manager, and they may not be appropriate for the job today. Each one must be questioned. Has the manager got the right skills, an appropriate number of people, the right systems to enable these people to do the work effectively and efficiently and so on?

In some cases, these working resources will be negotiated directly by the manager concerned with whoever supplies them—the Information Services Department, perhaps. For many of the resources, they will have to be negotiated with you or through you. If you really want to move the enterprise significantly forwards, expect the status quo to be challenged.

It is essential that your managers have the right amount of working resources to achieve the needed results, of course, but not too much, or the costs will be too high. Also, they must not be poor quality resources or the outputs will be correspondingly poor. This is where advice from you (and, possibly, coaching) can help your managers to determine what their exact needs are.

Now your managers have a precise description of the results you want, and what working resources are needed to deliver the results efficiently and effectively.

It is convenient to distinguish between these *working* resources and what we shall call *worked-on* resources. These are resources that pass *through* the manager's domain during the performance of the work. Working *on* these resources produces the outputs—the needed results. Their acquisition also has to be negotiated. They are not there semi-permanently, like the working resources. In general, the faster they move through the manager's domain, the better, in terms of costs and cycle times.

Obvious examples of worked-on resources are raw materials that are processed in the manager's domain to make a product—glue, detergent, camera film, sheet steel, for example. Others are components that must be acquired and assembled (by *working* resources, of course) to make a camera, a settee, a garden spade, a motor car, for example. Yet others are people who pass through an education or training programme. They are 'worked on' by the working resources of the manager concerned with education and training to produce the needed result—a well-trained sales representative, for example. A hernia patient leaves the hospital after a well-conducted admission, preparation, operation and after-care. You can actually watch these worked-on resources as they pass through the manager's domain.

Many jobs, though, involve worked-on resources that are largely invisible—information, for example. The needed *result* is an invoice, a holiday package, an approved loan, a marketing strategy, a legal brief, a price list, an income tax assessment and so forth.

When the correct working and worked-on resources have been identified, your managers cannot yet secure them until they have also identified the sources of supply. Then they have to negotiate to secure them. In the new world of peer-to-peer relationships, cross-functional processes and extended enterprises—to customers, external suppliers and alliance partners—the ability to negotiate well is a key skill for your managers (and you) to develop.

Check-list 12 is quite short. It summarizes what has been described above.

CHECK-LIST 12   The ability to secure scarce or vital resources

1 What are the results that are required?

2 What are the *working* resources needed to produce the required results?

3 What are the *worked-on* resources needed to produce the required results?

4 Who has, or can authorize, the supply of the needed resources?

You have responsibility for the first item, defining the results that are required. Your managers should individually address items 2, 3 and 4, with your help as needed.

There follow two examples to illustrate how this Check-list 12 may be applied. In the first, we assume that one of your managers has the responsibility for processing customer orders. We will assume that yours is a manufacturing company making items of capital equipment. Many other people in other parts of the company, and beyond, have an interest in this being done excellently. For example:

- *manufacturing* They need to know what to make, how many and when
- *marketing* They need to know which customers have which products installed and on order; which sales representatives are to receive commission and how much
- *procurement* They need to know which raw materials and components to order, and when they need to be available for manufacturing (this is particularly important in a Just-In-Time environment)
- *service engineering* They need to know what they have to install, and where and when it will be delivered
- *information services* They need to have very full details about the order to maintain accurate customer records for other users
- *finance* They need to know so that billing can be arranged, and to enable cash flow projections—in and out—to be prepared
- *education and training* They need to know in order to arrange any necessary education and training that may be necessary for affected customer or company personnel

- *distribution* They need to know what is on order, when and where it is to be delivered
- *alliance partners* They may need to know in case the order contains elements to which they make an essential contribution—software, for example
- *customers* They need to know to arrange power and water supplies, perhaps, to schedule staff training, building alterations, for example, and so forth.

Your manager has to take an even broader perspective of the business than you do, a perspective that may include some or all of the internal functions mentioned above. Also, your manager has given you a very clear idea (we assume) or told you to find out about the needs of the other functions who depend on the excellence of your order processing activities. This is to enable these other functions to keep *their* costs down and customer satisfaction high. So, you know the *results* that are needed from whichever of your managers is in charge of order processing.

Now we can go through Check-list 12 with answers for this example.

1 *Results* Customer order status is known to all who have a need to know from the day the order is placed until all payments have been received (we assume this is *not* the way things are today, otherwise as a future target it would be trivial).
2 *Working resources* This is not a new activity for the company. It has been going on for years now, but never to the total satisfaction of all of its 'customers'. So, we can assume that the basic working resources are there already—people, premises, heat, light and power and so forth. Now, with a rather more aggressive results target and a clear idea of all 'customer' needs, the old working resources must be re-assessed. New or modified necessary working resources might include:

- on-line order processing facilities and the necessary computer hardware, software and telecommunications
- the ability to provide order status information, on-line, to other parts of the company, to strategic alliance partners and to customers, which means more telecommunications facilities, of course
- enhanced skills of the people doing the work
- *fewer* people doing the work
- less space, but a different layout, different office furnishings, lighting and so forth.

If this seems unreasonable or impossible, you will have to modify the target to be somewhat more modest, then sell it to the 'customers'. *You* have to sell the inferior results, not the manager. After all, you set the targets.

3 *Worked-on resources* There is no physical product emerging from this activity. What does emerge is information. All of the *worked-on* resources are also information. They may include:

- customer information—who they are, where they are, whether the order is for an existing customer or a new one and so on
- previous order history
- what has been ordered, when
- How the order was placed—mail, via marketing, via an agent or dealer, on-line from the customer and so on
- where delivery should take place, when and how
- credit limits
- terms and conditions, prices
- whether this is a totally new product, a replacement or a product that is added on to an existing installed product
- where we shall be doing business in the future (this is needed to prepare for the day when orders start to come in from a new area with different currencies, delivery requirements, legal requirements, for example. The day these orders arrive is too late, so this point needs to be catered for now).

4 *Supplies* The new on-line system for order processing will probably be sufficiently expensive to need negotiating through you. Besides, its scope is so far-reaching and potentially strategic, you had better discuss it with your colleagues and other customers of the order processing activity. You will also no doubt be involved in the proposed headcount reduction.

The manager should be able to negotiate most of the *worked-on* resources, with a little help from you, perhaps. Suppliers within the company may include: Marketing, Legal, Information Services, Education and Training Departments and so forth. Suppliers *beyond* the company may include alliance partners, agents, dealers and real customers.

Notice that some *suppliers* also have an interest in the order processing activity being excellent. For example, the Marketing Department needs the process to be excellent in order to maintain accurate customer records and to pay the right amount of commission to sales representatives. Marketing, though, may also be a supplier of orders, and up to now their orders may have been late, incomplete and generally confusing. However, it puts the manager of order processing in a much stronger negotiating position for good inputs when this supplier is also a customer!

Now that you can see how this check-list works, we can keep the second example shorter. Here, we have assumed that the activity is to monitor legislative activity. There have been some unpleasant exposures in the past and some lost opportunities. You have framed a fairly tough target, as follows.

1 *Results* We know about all laws, regulations, codes of practice, customs and so forth that are relevant to the pursuit of our business wherever we operate.

There will be no nasty surprises in laws, regulations and so forth. This means that if they are nasty, but unavoidable, we shall know about them in time to be able to respond or react effectively. (This is from a company in the medical products manufacturing industry. This target was set by the CEO.)

2 *Working resources* With this new, demanding target, the major enhancement here is probably on-line access to legal abstracting services and the European Community legislation.

3 *Worked-on resources* The necessary inputs will include information concerning:

- which countries we do business in, where we will be opening up next and when
- what legal, religious, political, national, cultural, dietary, linguistic issues may affect us
- legislation, regulations, codes of practice
- what changes are coming and when
- what new opportunities are coming—lifting of trade sanctions, tariff barriers, Eastern Europe, lifting or imposition of currency controls, emerging possibilities in Iran, Africa, for example.

4 *Suppliers* Internal suppliers will include people concerned with product design, marketing, product planning and so forth, who are also key internal customers of this activity, of course. Most suppliers for this activity will be external, including:

- government agencies
- political lobbyists
- 'contacts' (let us leave it like that!)
- legal counsel
- translation services
- the media
- standards organizations
- trade associations
- consumer associations and so forth.

Notice that the required results in both examples are quite simple statements. They are sufficiently precise that you know when you have succeeded. The *means* by which the results are achieved are specifically excluded from the targets, leaving lots of scope for innovation. It is hard to deny the long-term relevance of these targets.

The ability to manage change

This is not only how good the manager is at coping with change, but also how well the manager's *people* can handle it. Even so, you may have the most enthusiastically flexible manager and personnel, but their feet are effectively set in concrete because of antique, inflexible systems, for example. More accurately, they are often trapped in yesterday's silicon— old computer systems that cannot easily be changed, if at all. Remember the unfortunate suppliers to Ford who were unable to stop themselves producing totally useless invoices? There are other inhibitors to flexibility, of course, mostly in other *working* resources. Be prepared for some quite expensive challenges to the status quo, or else expect a much lower ability to manage change.

In the check-list that follows, we begin with some factors related to personnel, then move on to issues related to working resources. As usual with these check-lists, you are encouraged to add other items.

CHECK-LIST 13   The ability to manage change

1 What environmental issues inhibit innovation:

- internal, such as the 'style' of the enterprise, its organization structure, conflicting goals
- external, such as politics, pressure groups, religion, culture?

(Expect your managers to want your help in addressing the above and similar issues.)

2 How many days of formal education/training do the manager and the manager's personnel receive each year?

3 Is there a formal mechanism for personnel to suggest improvements?
How quickly does the manager respond to such suggestions?
How are the good ones rewarded?

4 Are Quality Circles or similar groups established?

5 How quickly can the group respond to:

- new customer requirements
- new market opportunities

- new technology opportunities
- new offerings from external suppliers
- changes in legislation?

6 What *specialized* assets (working resources) are used:

- those with a low liquidation value (or none), such as application software, out-of-date machinery, out-of-date procedures. (These may have cost a fortune and been a triumph ten years ago, but now they are like a dead albatross slung around the neck of the manager concerned and they are often quite hard to get rid of.)
- those with high transfer or conversion costs, such as:
  - *specialists* These people are often difficult, even impossible to change, yet the new organization structures are demanding a much broader, more generalist approach and knowledge
  - *historic buildings* The time, cost and emotional energy needed to change the use of your delightful old manor house from an executive education centre to a software centre, for example, can be huge. Just re-wiring the place for modern telecommunications can be a daunting operation (and probably necessary anyway, even if you leave it as an executive education centre).

7 How old are the buildings in which the work is done? (There are more planning hurdles to overcome with historic or listed buildings, but quite ordinary old ones can inhibit change.)

8 Have the buildings got false floors and ceilings?

9 Have they got easily changeable partition walls?

You and your managers may not be able to do very much about some of the inhibitors to change in the short term, but somebody has to *start*. This is you again.

Some of the necessary changes will be more difficult than others. They all become extremely difficult if the manager's people are not enthusiastic participants. They are the key elements in the manager's ability to manage change. This takes us back again to the climate of trust, coaching, involvement in plans and so on that each of your managers must consider for effective results, even in a business-as-usual environment.

You should find it easier to negotiate the consolidated additional resources for your domain now, however, as well as special resources needed for a specific manager. You know all the internal customers of the activities within your domain. The consequences of you not delivering the needed results should be capable of assessment, by you and your internal customers. You should now be extremely well prepared to present your case and the options in terms of lower performance if these *necessary* resources and changes are not wholly provided or supported. This is not being threatening. It is simply presenting a complete and well-argued business case. A rarity.

In the newer organizational structures, such case-by-case arguing, particularly for major infrastructure resources, should not be necessary. In these, the top management team works *together* across the entire scope of the enterprise, or business unit, rather than fighting from the particular corner of the Finance, Research and Development, Marketing, Logistics or other Department.

The holistic approach at the top should enable resource allocation (within the limits of what is available) to be decided according to the needs of the enterprise, rather than the most persuasively argued case (or the loudest, or the most threatening or the most plaintive), function by function. It should thereby enable planning, funding and installation of the basic infrastructure resources needed by any enterprise—telecommunications, data resources, buildings, vehicles, office space, for example. Then *you* need only negotiate and secure those resources that are specific to your particular domain.

The case of the overwhelmed manager

Then there is Bruno, one of your managers. He is in serious trouble, constantly struggling to keep his head above water. There are vacant positions in his group. They are behind schedule. As soon as they think they have caught up, the computer system fouls up and they more or less have to start again from scratch. How long can this go on? Bruno and his people are exhausted.

When you look at your analysis of Bruno, from earlier check-lists, you find that his weaknesses are to do with external relations, clearly identifying his needs, getting sufficient resources for his projects and making sure that promises are fulfilled. He is constantly improvising, a victim of the wishes and whims of others, instead of pressing on with his own views and following them through. The situation would be totally out of control if it were not for Bruno's strengths. He is loyal, ambitious, not afraid of work. Despite all the setbacks, he maintains a good team spirit in his group.

Only yesterday he staggered into your office and said, 'We will *never* get the new system working properly! The computer people keep squirming and blocking and smothering me in jargon and acronyms. Standards have not even been decided. Resources seem to have been reallocated to other projects. The start date will have to be postponed for another six months. I can't go back and give my group this kind of message—again!'

Nevertheless, your view is that the project *must* be finished and the new system must be installed and running on time. How can you help? You can't just say, 'Well, fix it!' The man needs help, from you.

If we look at the factors impacting results (see Check-list 5, page 59), in the case of Bruno, we see something like this:

- efficiency   low, nothing to speak of is coming out
- effectiveness   equally low
- employee satisfaction   still high—miraculously
- ability to secure critically   low—for one thing, the computer support
  needed resources   is critical and it is not there, nor does anyone
             seem to know when it will be
- ability to manage change   this is just about all that Bruno is doing, though
             in a highly reactive way!

Using the worksheets in Check-list 7 (see pages 80-87), the way you did for Brenda, you may come up with a list of improvements for Bruno something like this:

- understand our company, different roles and how it will change
- negotiate, get resources and support from others
- manage, review and control projects
- be in control of several tasks simultaneously
- recognize the *essential* tasks in a world full of ambiguity
- manage his own time effectively
- use the company's decision processes
- implement decisions.

Now, what can you do to help, quickly?

First of all, give him a realistic view of the situation. Bruno is thrashing about and is too busy fighting for survival to be able to analyse what he is doing properly. The light at the end of the tunnel never gets any closer. He has to be made to understand that it never *will* get any closer unless he changes his ways.

One good thing, Bruno does not seem to be showing any symptoms of plateauing, except, perhaps, rage—with the computer people (and himself)—and his motivation and that of his group still seems to be high enough, though for how much longer?

Bruno needs two things, at least. First, the offloading of any non-essential tasks. This may be necessary, but it is not sufficient in itself. He also needs to improve his basic management skills in the area of time and resource management and the negotiation of resources. Otherwise, the time released by offloading non-urgent tasks will be absorbed in more thrashing around. Then, he might benefit from some external professional advice regarding the information technology side of the project. This looks like a case for coaching from you, plus some other ways and means.

There are probably some things that *you* can do without for six months from Bruno's department—those rather time-consuming statistics, perhaps? There may be others that are less than critical—a newsletter, for example. One or two people might moan about its absence, but you have to get the priorities right. Bruno must succeed.

Bruno must play his part in this, too. Give him a week to come back to you with a list of items of unnecessary work. He may need a little guidance on how to look, but insist that he finds something that is either not necessary or can be combined with another operation, say, to save time and effort. There might be some ideas in earlier check-lists. He should involve his people, of course. *They* will find something even if he does not. Motivation is still high, after all.

Then, you have to organize some formal training in the basic skills of which he appears to have a poor grasp. Naturally, he will say he is too busy, but he isn't really. This is why you have to give him a very clear picture of the reality of the situation right at the start. In parallel with this should be your coaching. You must have regular meetings and reviews with him while all this is going on.

Finally, it might be worth employing an information systems consultant to help him, someone who knows the technology, can communicate from a position of knowledge with the computer people and who also has project management experience. This should help Bruno in defining and communicating his requirements and negotiating a formal agreement with the Information Services Department. It also effectively offloads more work from Bruno's shoulders to give him time for reflection (essential!) and to learn.

You might look also for some education to give him a broader view of himself and his group in the total context of the enterprise. He needs to be unafraid of stating his needs, in a business context, and negotiating them successfully. Then, he must develop the concentration and stamina to see that agreements are implemented.

The goal is to get a successful result from this project *and* give Bruno the necessary skills and confidence to handle the next one well.

You should also consider giving him some specific personnel objectives, as a manager reporting to you. The check-list in the next section should be helpful in this. Its aim is to give you a large enough number of examples to stimulate your own thinking.

Setting objectives for managers

The whole idea of giving objectives is to make sure that everyone, managers and non-managers alike, is clear about *what* they are expected to achieve. Particularly for managers (and increasingly for non-managers) the *means* of achieving the objectives should not normally be too explicit. In other words, 'This is the *result* that I want. I leave it to you to *find the best means to achieve it.*' In all but the most highly structured tasks (which management is *not*), this allows for innovation to take place.

There are three main categories of objectives for managers. All of your managers should have at least one of each. The first category relates to the business results that you want from your domain. We have given two examples earlier, for processing customer orders and for monitoring legislative activity, respectively.

The second category relates to the manager's responsibility to ensure a smooth and efficient operation and to 'maintain the machinery', so to speak. There is no point in achieving spectacular results at the cost of a smoking ruin all around you; kamikaze is not a good business concept. It is also an opportunity to think beyond 'maintaining the machinery', however, and to encourage ideas that could make really huge improvements. Many of these ideas may be totally impractical today, but some of them may be absolute gems. *At least* encourage thinking beyond the boundaries of, 'This is the way we do things around here' (we referred earlier to 'paradigm shifts', see page 30). Give each manager an objective, working together with the manager's group, to come up with suggestions for improvement using the grid shown in Figure P4.1.

OPPORTUNITIES FOR CHANGE

	Current paradigm	*New paradigm*
Short term	**Fast payoff**	**Pilots**
Long term	**Do differently**	**Re-engineer**

Figure P4.1

There are four quadrants. Those in the left-hand column relate to improvements to the operation that can be implemented within the existing framework without too much challenge to the status quo. The upper left quadrant, 'fast payoff' is for ideas that could be implemented within a week, say, and which would produce an immediate benefit. A simple example might be to stagger the lunch break so that there is *always* someone present to answer customer queries, rather than an answering machine. Such ideas usually cost very little and have a very quick return.

The lower left-hand quadrant, 'do differently' is for improvements that will take longer to implement, may require investments in technology, education, and so forth. The payoff should be correspondingly bigger.

> Allied Dunbar, the UK financial services company, provides an example. It invested in 3500 Toshiba laptop computers and the development of the software to enable sales representatives to do a financial 'health check' while interviewing a prospective or existing client. Based on the answers to the relevant questions, the computer is able to produce a highly tailored, personal profile of appropriate insurance and other investment opportunities. Inexperienced sales representatives with the laptops were able to generate four times as much new business, on average, as experienced sales representatives without a computer.

The right-hand column is for what are sometimes called 'paradigm shifts'. These are dramatic challenges to the status quo. Throw away the rule book. Think crazy; the crazier the better.

The top right-hand quadrant, 'pilots', is for massive challenges to the status quo, but which are amenable to a pilot project. This is where you can make a relatively small investment with the objective of learning how to make the thing work in the full scale. These are not experiments. The objective of a pilot project is to secure knowledge—costs, technical and financial risks, time-scales to implement, impacts on personnel, on the organization, education and training needs and so forth. The idea is to learn enough to move into the lower right-hand quadrant and reap the really big payoffs.

> In the late 1970s, somebody in McKesson had the idea of giving away terminals to customers and paying for the telecommunications costs. Crazy? It probably sounded crazy at the time. But they did not flood the place with terminals and communications equipment. They probably started with six or so nice, friendly customers. A pilot project. What would be the cost of this pilot scheme? Not large. What would be the damage to the business after three months or so if it was not successful? Very small. Who would know if it was a disaster? Not many people. It was confined to a few McKesson people and half a dozen friendly customers.

However, as we described earlier, it was not a disaster. The business from pharmacists who had the terminal facility grew very quickly. Moreover, a lot of learning took place, sufficient to enable the originators of the idea to go to the senior management of McKesson with a well-argued case to fund the expansion of the facility.

This illustrates the need for a pilot project before moving into the really big investments needed for the big payoff. It has to be this way.

Can you imagine what the response of top management in the 1970s would have been if someone had come to the Boardroom with a mad scheme to give away thousands of terminals to customers and pay for the huge computing power and telecommunications costs needed?

The lower right-hand quadrant is for those crazy (but potentially wonderful) ideas for which a pilot project is not possible. This is re-engineering.

An example comes from Federal Express's package tracking system. Customers' packages are tracked at all stages of shipment. Hand-held scanners let drivers collect customer data at the pick-up point. Terminals in their delivery vans are linked directly to Federal Express's mainframe computers. This reduces delivery errors and allows drivers to identify delinquent accounts. Customers do not pay if the delivery is not on time.

The CEO designed the system. No part of it could work until it was all in place. It simply was not amenable to a pilot project approach.

You should also learn something about your managers and their relationship with their people using Figure P4.2. If there are no suggestions for improvement, or maybe only one, under 'current paradigm', perhaps you should be concerned. There may well be good reasons for such a response from a manager and the group, or it may be a case of group stagnation. Either way, it merits investigation.

The third category of objectives relates to the managers' responsibility to provide opportunities for the further development of their people. Unfortunately, it is common practice to give highest priority to the purely business-related objectives and neglect those related to the manager's personnel. This manifests itself in a short-term focus on 'the numbers'. Moreover, business-related objectives tend to be better defined and easier to track and measure. If the objective is missed, it is usually quite obvious.

However, enterprises are not run by machines and systems (not yet, anyway). Such things are part of the inanimate resources of the enterprise. We referred to the *super-critical* resources on page 36 of:

- management
- personnel
- skills

It is *their* quality that determines how well the inanimate resources are exploited to deliver the needed results, and they are much more long term. Exploit the inanimate resources; husband the super-critical human ones.

Setting personnel-related objectives

Up to this point we have concentrated on your responsibility to develop the quality of management *per se*, with a strong focus on the needed results and on the necessary skills and motivation of the *manager*. However, each of your managers *also* has a responsibility to manage the quality and skills of *their* personnel. For this reason, we want to underline the manager's responsibilities as a manager of people in this section. There should be a loud and clear signal from you that you care about these, consistently.

A new manager should have different personnel-related objectives to a manager with long experience in the particular job, whether or not the new manager has previous management experience. This is because a manager (like anyone else) passes through different phases after joining or creating a group.

Briefly, the first phase is characterized by learning and listening and integrating into the social fabric of the group—becoming accepted as a member. In the second phase, the manager can begin to add a more personal touch, can challenge existing methods, start trying new ideas. If the new member of the group—whether or not a manager—tries to be too innovative during the 'socialization phase', though, rejection of the new idea is possible and attitudes tend to become fixed. For the *same suggestion*, a reaction of, 'too clever by half' can become 'Hey, that's a good idea!' after total acceptance into the group (we discuss this in more detail later in Part 5 under 'Induction of new managers' page 158).

Any objectives should contain indicators so that both you and the manager know if and when the objective has been achieved. This applies equally to personnel-related objectives. Obviously, both you and the manager should agree measurements so that progress can be monitored. If you can't measure it, you can't manage it.

Study the check-list that follows and think about Bruno. What kind of personnel-related objectives might be given to him? Then do the same for Martin and Brenda, and for

Brenda's replacement, Michael, a totally new manager.

The first column contains possible areas of concern under a major heading, such as 'Organizing the manager's group', or 'Personnel development'. Typical questions related to the area of concern are in the second column. The third column contains examples of personnel-related objectives that could be given to address the specific questions related to the area of concern. In some cases, we have given examples of indicators that the objective has been realized, in square brackets. For example, a question related to 'Organizing the manager's group' might be 'Are the objectives of the group accepted by all members?' An appropriate objective for the manager might be, 'Organize group activity to agree on objectives.' ['Present the result to me.'] is the indicator that it has been done, and the means for you to evaluate how well it has been done.

CHECK-LIST 14   Personnel-related objectives

Organizing the group

Area of concern	Possible questions	Examples of objectives [and indicators]
Objectives of group	Are the objectives accepted by all members? Does the manager accept the consequences of changes in the manager's responsibility?	Organize group activity to agree on objectives. [Present the result to me.]
Organize change	Changed responsibility? Reduction of personnel? Increased span of control?	Design/create new organization. Pilot new principles. [Present proposal and plan.]
New methods	Is the group being reduced?	Propose and introduce new methods of working. [Present proposals and monitor results.]
Relations with unions	What is the manager's responsibility? How is cooperation today? Any specific problem areas?	Establish good relations with key people involved. [Negotiate agreement in specific areas.]

Area of concern	Possible questions	Examples of objectives [and indicators]
Job descriptions	Are they up to date and relevant?	Review all job descriptions. Create new job descriptions where appropriate.
Job levels	Are the present levels up to date and correct?	Make a case for promotion of A. N. Other. [Job description and job evaluation of A. N. Other approved.]
Hiring/staffing	Are there current or expected vacancies?	Identify candidates for the particular jobs. Prepare job descriptions for advertising internally and/or externally. Work with Personnel function to solve a specific staffing problem.
Building competence	What competence gaps exist? Does the group contain excess or unnecessary competence? Is there sufficient back-up in critical areas?	Produce a competence plan including how to release competence not needed. Negotiate agreements with groups for assistance, exchange of services, or back-up. [Show agreements or documents of understanding.]
Succession	Is there an identified candidate to succeed the manager? Candidates to succeed other key people?	Identify one or two candidates. [Show the succession plan and the preparation plan.]

Area of concern	Possible questions	Examples of objectives [and indicators]
Overtime	High overtime being worked? High compensation for overtime?	Show how overtime may be reduced by X per cent.
Workload	Are there imbalances in the group?	Plan for rebalancing of work. Change responsibilities and job descriptions. [Propose a plan that is acceptable to all parties.]
	Has the manager an unacceptably high workload?	Define tasks that can be delegated, and to whom. [Present plan. Monitor workload.]
Holidays	Any out-of-line situations —excessive holidays or holidays not taken?	Prepare holiday plans. [Monitor conformance.]
Resignations	Reasons for loss of personnel?	Departure interviews. [Document and present conclusions and recommendations.]
Staff plan	Is the manager familiar with the background and development needs of employees?	Make a personnel plan for the group—jobs, job levels, job rotation, training requirements, hiring requirements and so on. [Documented plan. Show status in monthly reviews.]

Area of concern	Possible questions	Examples of objectives [and indicators]
Development plans	Does each individual have a development plan? Is there a regular routine for planning and monitoring individual development? Are individual interests and wishes considered?	Make a development plan for NN. [Name, plan, dates.] Make a plan for all employees. [Present plan and results at monthly reviews.] Identify individuals with high potential. [Document and propose development plan.]
Job rotation	What is the history of this group? How many individuals have been in the present job for more than three years? Are special development opportunities being used?	Rotate BB to a new job. Find a special assignment development opportunity for PP.
Education	Does an education plan exist? Is the plan being implemented? Are internal and external education offerings being used?	Ensure education and training plans are carried out. [Present plan and results.]
New employees	How are new employees introduced to the manager's group?	Make an introduction plan for HH, including necessary contacts with other departments and so on.
Delegation as a development tool	How good is this manager at delegating?	Delegation is not only planned, it happens.

Area of concern	Possible questions	Examples of objectives [and indicators]
Performance reviews	Does the manager have formal performance-related dialogues with all personnel?	[Performance reviews 100 per cent completed by ../..]
Meetings	What is the nature, frequency and content of meetings?	Hold meetings with high participation at least once every ... [Copy of notice, agenda and minutes to me.] Inform personnel regularly about plans, status, projects and critical situations. Personal dialogues with all group members. [Summarize, as needed, in monthly reviews.]
Monthly review	Is it appropriate that the manager holds monthly review meetings with key members of the group?	Establish a routine for monthly review meetings. [Keep me informed on a need-to-know basis.]
Issues critical to the enterprise	Does the group identify with the enterprise view in potentially critical areas, such as mergers, acquisitions, restructuring and so on.	Inform the group. Present the enterprise's position. Check for acceptance.
Employee opinions	What are the present attitudes to work, the enterprise, managers, colleagues, plans, benefits and so on? Documented in opinion survey?	Check for understanding and acceptance. [Carry out agreed activities by ../..]

Area of concern	Possible questions	Examples of objectives [and indicators]
Objectives	Are the employees' objectives well defined? Are the objectives accepted?	Reach agreement with LL on objectives and performance requirements [Review objectives with me. Review objectives and performance quarterly.]
Team spirit	Is there a good team spirit?	Propose the means to improve team spirit via assignments, group rewards, special programmes and so on.
Rewards	Does the manager use rewards actively and imaginatively?	Record all rewards given. [Demonstrate that reward match desired behaviour.
Performance assessment	Is the manager generally too generous or too hard in assessing employee performance?	[Demonstrate that assessments match agreed performance standards.]
Personnel programmes	Does the manager use the personnel programmes of the enterprise on behalf of the group?	Employees have a clear understanding of personnel policies as they affect them. [Opinion survey results.]
Dissatisfaction	Is there dissatisfaction? What are the real causes?	Identify sources of dissatisfaction. Propose means to resolve [Monitor progress.]

> Over to you

Personnel Related Objectives

Bruno

Martin

Brenda

Michael

Here are some suggestions.

- *Bruno* (see page 130)
  - Review all job descriptions. Work with the group to identify tasks that can be dropped and how the work may be reorganized.
  - Identify management candidates.
  - Arrange a study tour for the group as a reward when the new computer-based system is installed.
- *Martin* (see page 64ff.)
  - The objectives of the group and each individual in it are understood and accepted by all.
  - There are clear job descriptions for all his people.
  - Regular meetings are held with the group—at least once per month.
- *Brenda* (see page 98ff.)
  - Identify key personnel in the group and show plans and actions for retaining them and keeping them motivated.
  - (One of Brenda's people has had a drug problem. Brenda has devoted a lot of time to the rehabilitation of this individual. You and she both believe she should continue the special relationship after she has moved on.) Allocate ten per cent of her time to the employee with the drug problem.
- *Michael* (Brenda's replacement)
  - Make a personnel plan for the group.
  - Present the enterprise's personnel policy and programmes to the management committee.
  - Involve the whole group in defining objectives, strategies and activities for the coming year. Figure P4.2 might form a useful framework for this.

It is too early to give the totally new manager an objective to identify suitable management candidates, even though you see the need for it. The above three personnel-related objectives are probably enough for the time being. Presenting the enterprise's policy to your management committee is a one-off activity. It will ensure that it is well-researched and understood by Michael, at least. Besides, some of your other managers may well have forgotten parts of it and could do with an update.

      If you look back to that first day a few weeks ago, when you removed the old bits of fluff and the paper-clips from your desk, then look at the amount of information you have accumulated using the check-lists, you will find that you have gone very quickly up the learning curve. We assume you have been building that essential climate of trust at the same time. This, and your stewardship, will never stop. Next, we shall move on to the activities of planning, acquisition and disposal of your management resource.

Stars get noticed

Failures get noticed

What about me
(and the other 80 per cent)?

PART 5

MANAGING THE QUALITY OF MANAGEMENT (II): PLANNING, ACQUISITION AND DISPOSAL

Planning the management resource

In Part 4, we focused on the stewardship processes on the assumption that you already have an existing team of managers reporting to you from the day you became a middle manager. It was therefore necessary for you to get quickly up the learning curve to manage the resource that you inherited effectively, and to start to build the necessary climate of trust within your domain as soon as possible.

Now that you have this pretty well in hand, we can look ahead. Looking ahead, anticipating the future, and getting ready for it are key management and leadership activities for you. We shall take a fairly simple case to illustrate this. It is over-simplified, of course, being much more orderly than real life is nowadays, but it makes the point.

Suppose you have six managers reporting to you. Assume each stays in the same job for an average of three years before moving on. It follows that:

- two newly appointed managers will need a lot of your support in their first year, so your main focus will be on the processes of introducing new managers
- two will be in their second year, so they should be running their groups very independently by now and your main focus will be on the stewardship processes
- two will be in their third year, probably at their peak in terms of delivery of results. They are the next ones to leave, so you must focus on the disposal processes for these two managers, ensuring an elegant departure from their current jobs and a smooth entry into their next role–promotion, retirement, a horizontal move, whatever.
- you must also focus on the acquisition processes, however, or you will not have the right people to replace them as managers.

You cannot acquire the correct resource, however, until you know exactly what you need. Will you want exact replicas of the two managers who leave? We doubt it. This is where the planning process comes in, which is not a very difficult task in the nice, orderly scenario we have described above.

Now, let us add some turbulence from the real world. Organizational structures are changing rapidly, as we have discussed previously. Changes of all kinds are endemic—markets, competition, technologies, legislation, relationships, politics, social, environmental, economics and so forth.

Will you still *need* six managers in three years' time?
Or nine? Or three? Or any?

What qualities must these managers possess in the future?

How will you manage the transition from six to nine?
Or, more likely, from six to three?

This is where your senior position not only gives you the broader perspective and the longer-term view, it also carries the responsibility to create alternative future scenarios. We are not suggesting that you sit down and predict the future accurately—if you can do that, you don't need this book—but you must define some probable future scenarios for your domain. If you don't, who will? (And don't say, 'The Planning Department'.)

Obviously, you cannot do it alone. You need to spend time with your boss and other members of the top management team to be aware of and understand the major business and structural changes that may be coming. You need to relate what you learn there to your colleagues, the other middle managers. You need to discuss with them how the business and structural changes will affect your mutual relationships and dependencies. The IBM ThinkPad example we described earlier (see page 29) illustrates the benefits of cooperating across traditional functional boundaries to produce an innovative, successful product—impossible under the old regime. And you will probably need close contacts with key suppliers, customers, strategic alliance partners, dealers and agents as well.

Even in the tranquil scenario we outlined earlier, the planning processes have to be good. When we add some real-world turbulence, it places even greater responsibility on your shoulders to get it right. You are a manager of change, and a *maker* of change above all else.

We can break down the planning process for the management resource into five major sub-processes:

1 describe the probable future organization structure
2 define the number of managers needed in your domain
3 define the attributes and skills of each needed manager
4 review the available management attributes and skills in your domain
5 define the 'delta' that has to be closed, that is, the gap between what is available and what is needed.

Let us consider these sub-processes one at a time.

Describe the probable future organization structure

Obviously, we do not mean that you have to *define* it for the whole enterprise, but you must get as clear an image as possible in order to be able to describe your domain and its relationship with the rest of the enterprise. This is not only a necessary task for you to do, it is also a splendid opportunity to get involved in the strategic thinking of the enterprise, to see and be seen. You cannot plan effectively without it. You cannot go on even to define the number of managers you will need. The following questions highlight some of the things you might wish to explore.

What will be the future shape of the enterprise?
Will it be hierarchical? Will it remain hierarchical, but flatter?
How many management layers will be removed?

What are the core business processes of the enterprise, those whose excellence distinguishes this enterprise from others? Which processes will remain and which will be outsourced?

Is there going to be a shift of emphasis in these core (cross-functional) processes? When? What contribution does your domain make to them?

Is the enterprise's style likely to change at the top? (Find out when your CEO is likely to retire. If it is next year, watch out for changes.)

Will the style change because of business pressures (or fashion?), maybe to a more project- or team-oriented style? How will this affect the organization and tasks in your domain?

Is the enterprise being 'extended' (out to customers, suppliers, alliance partners, for example)? What are the interfaces between your domain and the extended enterprise?

Define the number of managers needed in your domain
This really has to be done in association with the next point.

Define the attributes and skills of each needed manager
Now you know some probable scenarios for the shape of the enterprise in the future, and the role of your domain in it, you should be able to describe the management resources you need to make it work. Will it be better if you merge two of your existing departments? If so, what kind of manager is going to be needed? An innovator? An administrator? A great negotiator? One who is gifted at working with other people? A leader? A technical giant? Will it be better if you focus on your key business processes, demolishing your internal departmental walls, giving a key process to each of your managers? How many key processes have you got? What are they? What are the needed attributes of a good owner for each (different) process? An innovator? An administrator? A great negotiator? And so on.

Review the available management attributes and skills

By now, using the tools and check-lists in Part 4 you should have an excellent idea of what you have got. This does not mean that you will have the *same* set of skills and attributes next year, or whatever is your scenario's planning horizon.

You have to look at what you will have *then*, based on planned departures and the management development programmes you have for those who will still be with you.

Define the 'delta' that has to be closed

There are two components to the delta: numbers of managers, and their skills and attributes. So, you may find yourself with a surplus in numbers, but a deficiency in skills and attributes. This is probable in today's environment. On the other hand, you may have a surplus both in numbers and of skills, or the right skills and attributes, but not enough managers. This happens when enterprises 'down-size' too vigorously. Then they find themselves hiring back former managers and employees as 'consultants'.

If this seems like hard and tedious work, then brace yourself for it. Nobody else is better qualified to do it than you are. If you leave it to someone else to do (who, by the way?), they will get it wrong. It is a critically important activity for you to do well if you are to manage and improve the Total Quality of management.

Now that you know what you will need in the future, you can go back to your stewardship work and see whether you need to modify the management development plans you have made for the managers who will remain with you. Also, if you need to acquire additional managers, move on to the next section, which deals with acquisition processes.

Acquiring the management resource

About 60 per cent of the desirable attributes must exist *before* the manager is first appointed. This means that education and training, job experience, coaching from you and so forth, can make improvements, but they are not the main source of management competence. They come embedded in the person on the day of appointment. This highlights the importance of the acquisition processes. If you get these wrong, the consequences can be long-lasting, deeply painful, damaging and expensive. You can't make a silk purse out of a sow's ear.

The desirable attributes of a management candidate can be divided into three categories:

1 what the candidate *has*–education, experience and so on
2 what the candidate *is*–creative, spontaneous or whatever
3 what the candidate *does*–delegates well, develops others, for example

At recruitment time, you should look particularly for what the candidate has and is. Of these, the 'has' attributes are the easiest to identify and confirm. The 'is' factors are often related to personality traits, which are harder to pin down (but see John Hunt's book, *Managing People at Work*, McGraw-Hill, 1992) and are not easily modified.

In contrast, the 'does' factors are what you can observe, measure and develop in the job. For practical purposes, the first 12 worksheets of Check-list 7, 'Worksheets for developing managers' (see pages 80–87) can be used to improve the 'does' attributes. Worksheet 13 is more of an 'is' list, more valuable as a means of evaluating your existing managers to ensure that they have the right personality traits for their present and future jobs. Middle managers may need additional education and training to do this evaluation well. An alternative is to use external consultants, with their specialized skills and personality tests.

When recruiting for a *particular* management job, it is useful to define three different competencies:

1 *threshold competencies* The manager cannot lack these completely–they have to exist at the beginning, at least to a certain degree, or failure is likely–and typical examples are presentation skills, stamina and so on
2 *today's key competencies* These are vital to success in the present job, for example team building, setting objectives, self-confidence and so on
3 *tomorrow's key competencies* These are crucial if you are to develop *your* domain to ensure its continued success, for example, establishing a creative climate, working across functional boundaries and so on.

The middle manager's responsibility is to find the right mix of today's and tomorrow's key competencies, while making sure that the threshold competencies exist to a sufficient degree.

However, your first questions when a management vacancy occurs (or you know that it *will* occur) is this: 'Should this management job be eliminated, or combined with other jobs?' You have to justify the continued existence of the job.

There are two strands to the processes of acquiring the management resource. One starts with the managers you have today. Knowing the future requirements of your domain, from the planning process, what can you do with your existing resources to prepare them for the future? We have covered this in some detail in Part 4.

The second strand of the acquisition process is concerned with *recruitment* of managers to meet the future requirements of your domain. Candidates may already be managers in another part of the enterprise, or they may be entirely outside the enterprise.

Equally, you may be offering the job to someone who has never before been a manager. Either way, you have to get it right.

We are not going to debate the pros and cons of internal management recruitment as a practice or a policy, nor will we debate the use of consultants, though, they can help by presenting you with a possibly longer list of candidates, and they tend to do quite deep personality and personal profile studies. Here, we shall focus on the attributes of your candidates, the things that you, personally, have to look for.

There is a large body of published information on the subject of selecting suitable management candidates, and all kinds of techniques for identifying potential strengths and weaknesses. Despite this, we still see large numbers of totally unsuitable people being appointed as managers. On page 3 we mentioned Peter Drucker's thoughts on the flattening of organizations. He was interviewed in the *Harvard Business Review* of May–June 1993 and said that, in his experience, only a third of promotions succeed. The remaining two-thirds are either, 'outright disasters or a nagging backache'.

We have no magic techniques to add to the large corpus of literature on the subject of recruitment, just some observations that may help you in the new, changing environment in which you will be working.

First, look at the *situation* into which you will be appointing the new manager. Is it one that requires a strong, cool, controlling hand? Is it one that needs the creativity and style of an entrepreneur? Is it a down-sizing situation, requiring very sensitive handling of the people in the group? Is it one that needs an injection of change and excitement (the replacement for Brenda, perhaps?).

Then, look at the prospective manager's group. Are the people there well-established, experienced and highly skilled? Is it a totally new group or a merging of two former groups?

Look at the manager's predecessor. Do you want an exact replica, to preserve continuity, to maintain the results, or do you want a dramatic change in style, as in the case of Brenda's group, perhaps?

Identifying new management potential

Clearly, if equal opportunities are prescribed by legislation, by union agreements or by the basic values and beliefs of your enterprise, they must be reflected in your procedures for identifying new management potential. One commonly perceived problem, at the time of appointment, is that there are not sufficient numbers or quality of women or minority group candidates. You may find that you have to give special focus to identifying, supporting and developing such candidates (we will get back to this in the next section, 'Making better appointment decisions').

Even if your enterprise sometimes recruits managers from outside, you should always have a good internal list of potential managers. It should be an objective for each of your managers to identify which of their people have management potential. Your managers will need to know just what this means today, in your enterprise. They should understand what the desirable attributes are as a result of your planning processes. Your additional responsibility is to ensure that the list of potential managers is debated and kept up to date. You also have to ensure that relevant development activities are in place and being followed (see Check-list 14, 'Personnel-related objectives', page 137).

Your list should be open to any other senior manager in the enterprise, and theirs must be open to you. This is necessary to enable the best possible cross-functional or enterprise-wide teams to be created.

If you recruit a manager from outside, you usually take great care in identifying and specifying your requirements. An external consultant will probably demand even greater detail. You will be communicating with people who have little or no knowledge of you and your enterprise. Promotion from within is not easier. The difficulties are different, that is all. The fact that the candidate as well as the job and the enterprise should be well understood seems to be an advantage, on the face of it. It has the disadvantage of the risk of following a too well-established path. The status quo remains.

Some enterprises have a formal, documented management profile. Again, this has a potential pitfall when you check candidates against it. If you are a slave to the profile, you may miss seeing what is unique to this situation, with this group of people, at this point in time. As the middle manager, you are close enough to the action to see exactly what is needed in a given situation.

Brenda's case illustrates what we mean. Before her arrival, the situation may have been almost chaotic. She established order, introduced new methods and practices that were sorely needed. Everything is now running smoothly. However, the business situation demands a leader who can produce new ideas and create an environment in which everyone in the group contributes. A 'good' candidate according to the documented management profile could be wrong *here*. It can only be a guideline. Your local judgement must prevail. You know all the parameters needed to make the right fit.

Making better appointment decisions

We shall summarize some of the desirable characteristics later, those things we believe managers *must* have in today's (and tomorrow's) world. We shall start by looking at some characteristics that *no* good manager should have.

If a candidate has any one of them, be very careful about going further. If a candidate has two or more, don't do it.

The first deadly sin is *difficulty in adapting to change*. There is not normally a single indicator of this, but if a candidate has a consistent history showing some or all of the following, you should be suspicious:

- not listening to other people
- not keeping promises
- having preconceived ideas, and sticking to them, no matter what
- manipulation of facts
- opportunism
- action without proper reflection, 'shooting from the hip'.

Beware of words of praise from such a person's current manager, who will be wanting to move the person on. Instead of the above, you may hear words like 'powerful', 'doesn't suffer fools gladly', 'courageous' and so on.

The second deadly sin is *low self-confidence*. Revealing signs here are:

- is easily disheartened
- does not participate in discussing important subjects of common interest
- avoids risks
- constantly seeks the support of others
- easily loses concentration.

The third deadly sin is *poor social skills*. Look for signs that this person:

- claims the praise, even when others deserve it
- manipulates other people
- is judgemental
- uses rumours, gossip and hidden agendas
- does not keep confidences
- thinks in terms of tasks, not people.

There are many splendid attributes for you to look out for, but these are three to avoid. The problem is that it takes time to build up such a pattern of knowledge about a person. Organizations using this technique say that management candidates have to be observed regularly over a year or two, and by more than one observer. You can start now. Consider giving all of your managers the job objectives of identifying and developing people with management potential. Then you and your managers can start the monitoring process.

If you think that this is too long term and rather intrusive, consider again the consequences (to all) of making the wrong management appointment.

Another revealing negative characteristic is the search for more and more precise job objectives. Any manager (or prospective manager) wanting such a high level of precision should be viewed with suspicion. Why is such precision *wanted*? It could be another sign of difficulty in adapting to change. 'Now I know exactly what I have to do, I can get on and do it, then claim my reward' (even though the need and circumstances may have changed?) It could also be a sign of low self-confidence. Tight precision in job objectives limits the range of possibilities for being creative on the part of the manager. It also defines a much narrower field for innovation and for the ideas that should be encouraged to flow up from the manager's people.

Beware the workaholic. Workaholics tend to want to do everything themselves, 'to make sure it gets done right!', you hear them say, and they tend to be poor at delegating anything except the most trivial tasks. As managers, they often expect their people to put in the same ridiculously long hours that they 'work'. The personnel do not get the interesting and challenging jobs, of course. The boss does these. The result can be lack of initiative, lack of imagination and poor productivity, despite the busy appearance—the early start and the lights on until late at night while they wait for the boss to go home, at last.

Should you ever deviate from the principle of appointing the 'best' person for the job? This takes us back to the equal opportunities question. If your need, or objective, is to increase significantly the number of women managers, for example, or local people or a specific ethnic group as managers, you may need role models who demonstrate that such development is possible and who also serve as a source of inspiration for the rest of the particular population. It is not a matter of meeting a specific percentage because you *still* have to find the best person—the best person for the enterprise *and* for the particular job. As a middle manager, you must make and accept such long-term decisions. Not only that, you will also have to make extra efforts, if necessary, to ensure the successful development of this person.

Now, let us turn to the essential attributes of excellent managers.

CHECK-LIST 15   The imperatives of good management candidates

1   Look out for candidates who have a good track record of successful implementation, rather than just an ability to create superb plans. Look for performance rather than credentials; 'This is what I can *do!*' rather than, 'This is what I know'.

You will be told wonderful stories about achievements. Check them. Were tangible results delivered? Were the projects properly completed? What still needs to be done? What problems were encountered and how were they solved?

2   Look for a record of making decisions rather than recommendations. Teamwork is right for many decisions, but decision-making ability is one of the most important attributes for a manager to have.

3 Look for people with intellectual curiosity, who ask about (or know about) what is happening in adjacent and distant parts of the enterprise and in its environment, in the widest sense. You need people who can integrate a totality. It is no longer possible to manage by looking at one particular part only.

4 Any management candidate today must be computer literate. Anyone who is disdainful about information technology is already a managerial dinosaur. Like it or not, information technology is critically bound up in the key business processes of your enterprise—or it very soon will be.

Information technology is the enabling technology that supports down-sizing, delayering, business transformation or 're-engineering', extending the enterprise out to customers, suppliers and alliance partners, the move to cross-functional process management to reduce costs and decrease cycle times and so on. You and your managers *must* be capable of using the information technology resources effectively. At least as important, you have to be actively involved in directing information technology and managing its influence on your domain and beyond. Information technology is much too important to be left to the technicians.

5 Naturally, look for signs of leadership. Look for them not only in work—projects and so forth—but also at home, in sports, military service, local government, charity work and so on.

6 Look for any signs that may show a natural gift for working with other people. Listen for examples that show the candidate prefers working with others to being a lone wolf. Hobbies and sports activities can be revealing here, too. Again, if spectacular past achievements are claimed, find out whether it was a group effort or whether the others were mere spectators.

7 Look for the ability to cope with misfortunes. How did the candidate respond to broken promises, family problems, catastrophes at work, cancelled projects and so forth. If you have someone who claims to have succeeded at everything in life, you are either facing a liar or someone who lacks some vital, normal human experiences.

These are the compelling attributes to look for, Then, find out what *motivates* this person to want to be a manager. What *kinds* of situations are brought up as examples of excellent performance? What recurring themes can you detect? Is this someone who wants to be at the centre, taking the lead, or someone who prefers to work alone and come out with a perfect result? Are there predominant patterns for creating new ideas, acquiring power, spontaneity or structure? Is this a street-fighter or someone who needs to be loved by other people?

Then, perhaps, you can match the attributes to the job, with a higher probability of success than Peter Drucker's observed third. Most managers today are still appointed entirely on their track record of business expertise or success in a non-supervisory role. This is why Drucker sees two-thirds as failures. Or is he being too kind?

Induction of new managers

We have included this topic with acquisition processes rather than stewardship because, whereas you have the *person* on Day1, you have not got an effective *management resource* until induction has been successfully completed. This applies to experienced managers moving into a new job within your domain just as much as for newly appointed managers. There are some differences for newly appointed managers, however, which we shall discuss later.

Induction applies to all employees. We have all experienced it a number of times. It makes it all the more strange that it is usually so badly done. Yet, an employee or manager cannot be properly productive–delivering the needed results–until it has been completed. You can accelerate the process of induction, but you cannot avoid it.

We shall look at some basic principles regarding the changing relationship between any individual and the job, and with the other people in the person's group and its surroundings. Then, we shall focus on those that are specific to managers, and particularly on those affecting you as a manager of managers. We have already looked at some of the manifestations in the later periods of working in the same job in the section on plateauing (see pages 100–109). Here, we concentrate on the phases *before* that, particularly right at the beginning.

It may seem paradoxical, but you should start *before* the beginning, if the beginning is the starting date of the manager's new job. The *real* beginning is when the prospective candidate first becomes aware of the possibility that they might be given the new job. This is when images and impressions begin to form. They should become much clearer during the interview and other selection procedures.

The more the successful candidate emerges with a clear, complete and accurate picture, the better for the induction processes. This steady build-up of what the reality actually is should continue right up to the time the manager starts the new job. Then, circumstances will cause it to accelerate. So, the better the stock at the beginning, the better for the manager and the manager's group.

If you doubt it, take 20 minutes and try this. It is called The Blind Walk. Go outside with a colleague, to the car park, the road, anywhere. Blindfold yourself so you can see absolutely nothing. Then, your colleague simply walks you around for ten minutes. It will seem like eternity. Your 'guide' can communicate in any way they like with you, but you must not be able to *see* anything. After ten minutes, change the roles. Then discuss what it felt like to be blind.

In your guiding of the blindfolded person, you will find that you improve rapidly over the ten minutes. You will notice how totally vulnerable and dependent on you the blindfolded person is, how nervous and afraid of moving confidently forwards they are. You will miss pointing out things that are obvious to you, at first, because you can see them. But the lack of this information can cause hesitation or even panic for the person you are leading— standing on a tiny pebble, moving from tarmac to a grass surface, even a slight change of slope upwards or, even more terrifying, down, for example. After a few minutes, you will be describing in much richer detail what lies just ahead *and* what will be coming up in a few paces—a low wall, a grassy bank, a hedge on the left, a turn to the right. As you get better at describing what lies ahead, you will *feel* the much greater confidence of the person you are leading. After ten minutes, you will probably both be striding out quite confidently.

If you start as the blindfolded person, when you change roles and become the guide, you will be much better at it from the beginning. (You *should* start as the blindfolded person, by the way.) You will have learned a lot about what your needs for information and support are from the previous ten minutes. Do not tell your former guide about the observations we have made in the preceding paragraph. Let the new blindfolded person find out for themselves!

The message is this: *the new job starts from the day the candidate knows about it.* Only one candidate gets the job, of course, but the clearer the image of what lies ahead is—the expectations, everything—the better equipped the manager will be to move confidently forwards on Day 1. You cannot afford the time and cost of flinging people in at the deep end to flounder about, trying to find even the basic rules of survival in their new environment. People who have unrealistic views and expectations are liable to encounter a severe 'reality shock' when they confront the true demands of the job. This reality shock is not only painful, it gets in the way.

Ralph Katz has studied the relationship between an individual and the job, and the job setting, while he was at the Massachusetts Institute of Technology. It gives us a useful framework to apply to your managers.

Katz believes that there are three different phases that we all pass through. The first, he calls 'socialization'. It happens every time someone changes jobs, whether they are a new recruit, have transferred or been promoted. This is the period when you learn what is normal, acceptable behaviour in the group, what is appropriate and expected, the language and jargon of communication, what is funny and what is not funny, how the reward system actually works, what the expectations of your manager are. Further, all of this is *necessary*, in addition to learning the technical requirements of the new job. The more dramatic the change of jobs, the more intense can be the socialization experience. Think of someone moving from Manufacturing to the Marketing Department, or from the Sales to the Accounts Department, for example. Yet, *exactly* such moves will become desirable and happen much more frequently in the successful, flexible enterprises of the future.

People in the socialization phase have a high dependence on others around them. They need it to define and interpret exactly what is going on. This real *need* for dependence makes the individual highly susceptible to influence from others in the group. So, you have to watch out for the battle-scarred, embittered veteran who plateaued years ago and sees an opportunity to attract a new recruit to the veteran's miserable clique: 'Come and have a cup of coffee and I'll tell you how things *really* work around here. And don't take any notice of that idiot. I've seen three or four managers come and go here. They're all the same!' It can take a very long time to change this 'image of reality', coming as it does when the individual is so malleable and susceptible.

Of course, if you and your managers are doing a good job, there will not be any embittered, battle-scarred veterans around. However, do recognize the inevitable need for dependence in the socialization phase, and provide the right kind. The better prepared the candidate is, of course, the lower the need. But the need still exists.

This socialization phase can be as short as a month or as long as a year, depending on the nature of the job. The more unstructured and non-routine the job, the longer it will take. Unfortunately, this describes the job of management. So, look for means to hurry it along, but be patient.

Katz calls the second phase 'innovation'. The social context of the workplace is now in place, the individual is accepted and respected by the others in the group, by subordinates, by superiors, so energies can be devoted to the job. There is much less dependence on others. Acceptance of the individual means that innovation can take place and will be treated with respect, even admiration. Too much 'cleverness' displayed early in the socialization phase can lead to its rejection, even if it is relevant and good. This is another reason for accelerating this phase as much as possible (it means the newly appointed individual has to be patient, too).

Katz's third phase is called 'stabilization'. This is where we run into the dangers of plateauing that we discussed earlier (see pages 100–109). Enthusiasm may wane and what used to be challenging and exciting may no longer hold any interest at all. This is when there is a danger of total inflexibility, and worse, selective perception of information and events. You see only what you want to see, even in the face of compelling evidence to the contrary, such as the consequences of a bad decision earlier.

We know that it is not necessary to suffer in this phase. It is up to you and your managers to maintain the challenge and excitement of the job. Then, you will be rewarded by continued growth and innovation.

- *Shorten* the socialization phase
- *Prolong* the innovation phase
- *Avoid* the negative aspects of the stabilization phase.

The new organization structures should help considerably in prolonging the innovation phase by providing a richer set of opportunities for new challenges. On the other hand, the constant flux means that groups, teams and project members will usually be together for a shorter period of time than in the more stable regimes of the past. This makes effective management and acceleration of the socialization phase even more important if these groups are to produce effective results, fast.

Now that we have a general structure, we can use it to be more specific and consider the induction of *managers*. In particular, how can you get a manager quickly and effectively through the phase of socialization and also ensure that they are better prepared for the phase of innovation?

One difference between managers on appointment to a new role and non-managers is immediately obvious. For non-managers, the critical group for socialization, for dependence, for establishing the working context, is the non-manager's new colleagues. They share the same working space, tasks and so forth. They are probably together for most of the working day.

A manager has two critical groups with whom the first phase must be passed successfully. First, is the manager's new personnel—Brenda's old group in the case of Michael, her replacement. Second, the manager's peers—the other managers who report to you. Then there is you, and other peers of the manager in other parts of the enterprise and beyond, and top management, perhaps. In the immediate work context, we shall focus first on the manager's new group, and then on your other managers as a group. Another difference is that the manager typically does not spend most of the working day in the midst of *either* group. In the future, even the manager's own personnel will be more invisible than in the past, working with customer teams, or on projects in other parts of the enterprise.

In relation to the manager's new group, by far the most important element of the socialization phase is to build the climate of trust. When this has been established, the manager *and the group* can effectively move forwards together into a new phase of innovation. The group has a leader. This is what seems to be needed for Brenda's group. In the case of Martin, the climate of trust has apparently never been established. Results are being produced, but how much better would they be if Martin and his team were able to innovate and work effectively *together*?

There is not much you and the manager can do before Day 1 about actually *building* the climate of trust. Building it depends on the group's perception's of the manager's *predictability, clear communications, relevance, consistency, fairness* and *visibility*. These can only be judged according to the manager's actions *after* Day 1. But you can help the manager to get ready for it. Let the manager read the section 'The climate of trust', page 71, for example. Then plan some coaching from you to ensure that it is done well. This should be easier for Brenda's replacement, in principle, than for Martin; your task there is much more difficult because he is starting from a negative position.

The lessons from The Blind Walk apply to the manager's new group as well as to the manager. *They* will spend time thinking, wondering and talking about their new manager before Day 1, just as the new manager spends time thinking about *them*. Will there be changes of style, working methods, reward systems, leadership, organization within the group, new tasks, reallocation of work, and so on? What is the new manager like as a *person*? What is the new manager's background, experience, track record? What qualified this person for the job?

Here again, you can do *some* preparation of the ground, but gently. You have *your* perception of this new manager, as a manager, and it is a good perception or you would not have made the job offer in the first place. Beware of raising expectations too high in the manager's new group, however. One slip during the socilization phase, before some successes has been achieved and before the climate of trust has been developed, and the high expectations can be shattered.

When we consider the other critical group in terms of the socialization phase—the other managers who report to you—the new manager will typically spend even less time with them, but they will usually be important in terms of mutual dependencies for achieving results, theirs and the new manager's. You can probably do rather more before Day 1 with this group, to help things along.

> The Swedish furniture giant, IKEA, has an interesting approach to this. It uses consensus decisions within management committees on any new manager to be taken into the group. When all concerned managers agree on a candidate, each one of them pledges to do their utmost to make the new manager succeed.

The check-list that follows is a long one. It includes all kinds of things that normally have to be in place for a manager to function effectively. Some of them are fairly boring administrivia, but needed none the less. Some may not be appropriate in your enterprise. Some things may be missing from our list that may be needed where you work. As usual, regard it as a starting point to prune to your own requirements, adding your own ideas.

Some items are specific to someone being appointed a manager for the first time. Others are more relevant for a management appointment from outside the enterprise.

Try using the check-list to identify those items that might help the manager taking over Brenda's group to pass through the socialization phase. Assume that the manager is appointed from within the enterprise, from outside your own domain, and that this is *not* someone who is totally new as a manager. The basic management skills are there, and the culture and style of the enterprise are known.

First, identify which items could help the socialization phase *before* Day 1. Distinguish between those that might help in relation to Brenda's old group and those that are more relevant to relationships with the rest of your managers, and others. Again, *don't try to 'boil the ocean'*. There is only a certain amount of time and opportunity available. Select only those things that will have the biggest impact from the time the offer is accepted up to Day 1.

Then, identify which items should help the socialization phase *after* Day 1. By all means, look again at the section 'The climate of trust' (see page 71), for completeness, and our recommendations under 'Coaching managers' (see page 95).

CHECK-LIST 16   Induction of a manager

1 Announcement and so on:

☐ introduce to the manager's new group
☐ update personnel files
☐ update distribution lists
☐ document sign-off authority
☐ announce the appointment to the manager's peers
☐ welcome to your management committee
☐ announcement within the enterprise
☐ press release, if appropriate
☐ announcement to external customers and other key people
☐ personal introduction to customers and other key people.

2 Policies and so on of the enterprise:

☐ culture and values; their implications in real life
☐ personnel policy
☐ the way we view customers, internal and external
☐ the way we view quality
☐ what kind of people we want to hire
☐ our view of performance assessment
☐ policies and practices for travelling; domestic and abroad
☐ how we use reward and motivation programmes
☐ how we relate to the media, government, trade associations and so on.

3 The manager's job:

☐ where the job fits into the total organization
☐ job description
☐ the manager's key internal and external customers, and their expectations
☐ other departments; key internal and external suppliers
☐ key individuals
☐ information systems on which the manager will depend
☐ quality status, quality targets

☐ business and personnel objectives for the next period
☐ special requirements for this job
☐ budget responsibility; current position
☐ current plans for the manager's group
☐ urgent problems
☐ personnel files and information
☐ has the predecessor conducted all concluding performance reviews?
☐ special personnel situations or cases
☐ job descriptions, development plans, career plans for all personnel
☐ responsibility for premises, equipment, systems
☐ responsibility for safety and security, work environment
☐ responsibility for confidential and sensitive information
☐ environmental issues, pollution and so on
☐ plan management development
☐ plan other personal development for the new manager
☐ the manager's personal plan for the near future.

4 The way we work:

☐ annual planning processes—key dates
☐ regular meetings of the management committee—dates, responsibilities
☐ budget planning and follow-up
☐ information systems developments
☐ salary planning
☐ formal reports—contents and timing
☐ meetings or committees the manager must attend
☐ recruiting and hiring procedures
☐ promotion planning
☐ education planning
☐ relationships with unions and others similar bodies
☐ control of working hours, overtime, holidays and so on.

5 How we will work together:

☐ monthly reviews or other regular meetings with you
☐ typical agenda
☐ 'grandparent' review by you, before and after the manager's performance reviews with personnel
☐ who signs-off what (travel, purchases and so on)?
☐ salary adjustments.

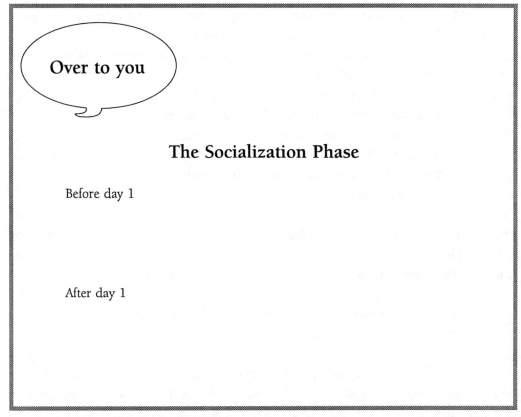

Over to you

The Socialization Phase

Before day 1

After day 1

As usual, there is no 'correct' solution because we do not know enough about Brenda, her group, what they do or what is the kind of enterprise where they work. The following is a fairly colourless suggestion, of necessity.

Before Day 1

1 *Introduce to the manager's new group* This way, faces can be put to names right at the start. We suggest that the meeting be fairly brief and formal, *not* followed by inordinate consumption at a local hostelry, for example. This may be fine for a departure, but not (normally) for an introduction. If yours is a brewing or whisky distilling business, however, it may be different.

    If Brenda already knows her replacement well, she can probably do the introduction better than you, particularly if hers is a positive and amiable departure, which it should be (see 'Disposal of the management resource' on pages 169–178 to make sure that it is.)

2 *Announce the appointment to the manager's peers* Let them know as soon as possible, at your management committee meeting, or by memo, if this would be quicker.

3   *Welcome to your management committee* If there is an opportunity before Day 1, have the new manager attend one of your meetings. If it is normal to have a convivial continuation after the formal business, fine. Expectations will then be known and experienced.

4   *Personnel files and information* The manager has met the new group. Now, their individual performances, skills, background and so on can be studied.

5   *Special personnel situations and cases* Remember that one of Brenda's people has had a drug problem and she will continue the special relationship after she has moved on. The new manager needs to know about this rather tricky situation as soon as possible.

This is about all, before Day 1. In a real-life situation, other items may be critically important, depending on the nature of the job and the enterprise. For a situation where the appointment is for a regional sales manager, for example, it may be important to add:

- announcement to external customers and other key people
- personal introduction to customers and other key people.

Remember, we are considering only those items that can help the socialization phase. All of the other things will have to be done—and more, no doubt. But *after* Day 1, probably the most important thing you can do is help the manager to build a climate of trust.

For a manager appointed from *outside* the enterprise, the same considerations apply, but, additionally, you should consider some of the items under 'Policies and so on of the enterprise' in Check-list 16. For an outsider, coming to terms with these as soon as possible is an important part of the socialization processes.

A new manager's development

For a totally new manager, the same considerations also apply, but there must, additionally, be the development of basic management skills. The sooner the better.

If your enterprise has a formal education programme for newly appointed managers, you probably went through it yourself. How long ago? When was the last time you looked at its content? How can you send a newly appointed manager on a course about which your knowledge may be sketchy or even totally out of date? Find out what it is like now. Call the manager in charge of the programme and get a description of the course contents and structure, at least. Then, get the new manager to present to you what the main learning points were, the strengths and weaknesses of the course, after attending it. This way, you will know your starting point for future development.

A suggested outline for education and training of new managers is as follows:

- legislation, rules, regulations and company programmes
- managing people
- leading teams
- personal development.

We suggest that all managers should go through the first three items. Personal development should be individual, depending on the manager and the requirements of the job. After you have a clear understanding of the formal new manager induction course, you can plan what needs to be done. The following check-list includes some suggested detail for these four headings. Use it and add to it for your own specific situation.

CHECK-LIST 17   A new manager's education and training

1 *Legislation, rules, regulations and company programmes:*

☐ legislation and union agreements in the labour market:

- ◼ types of employment
- ◼ working hours, overtime, holidays, leave of absence
- ◼ environmental and safety issues and so forth

☐ personnel policy
☐ personnel programmes:

- ◼ salary programmes
- ◼ performance appraisal
- ◼ other processes, routines, forms, systems and so forth.

2 *Managing people:*

☐ management and leadership
☐ situational leadership
☐ motivation
☐ equal opportunities

☐ setting objectives
☐ delegation
☐ personnel development
☐ rewards
☐ handling difficult situations:

■ unsatisfactory performance
■ presenting unpopular management decisions/policies
■ alcohol and drug abuse and so forth.

3 *Leading a team:*

☐ group dynamics
☐ team spirit
☐ creating effective teams
☐ resolving conflicts.

4 *Personal development:*

☐ negotiation skills
☐ presentation skills
☐ effective writing
☐ planning
☐ project management
☐ decision making
☐ creativity
☐ time management
☐ foreign language development
☐ working with cultural differences and so forth.

You should want managers who have a broad view of the enterprise and its environment. So, ideally, the programmes that address these different items should include dialogues with top management and other senior managers from all over the enterprise. This applies whether the courses are run and staffed in-house or whether they are run on a one-company basis by a business school, for example. There is a double benefit in having these senior management dialogues. The participants have a chance to hear the more strategic viewpoints straight from the top. The people at the top have a chance to find out what is really going on. There are no filters in either direction. Some time ago, a senior vice-president of one American company sold the idea of such dialogues in the company's management development programme entirely for this reason. He saw it as just about the only legitimate means of bursting through the insulating layers of staff people in order to get to where the work was really done. Most of these layers are extinct now. If you use external courses for your new managers where other participants from other enterprises are also present, there is no opportunity for dialogues with top management. You will have to ensure that your new managers are given such contacts by other means.

Particularly for a manager appointed for the first time, coaching from you is an important tool for development. For example, one area where your support will be helpful is performance assessment or performance reviews. The new manager will never before have been in the manager's seat. The manager may be nervous and, as a result, may be happy enough to get to the end of the meeting with almost *any* kind of agreement. This represents a lost opportunity to get the thing right and have a mutually clear understanding of the employee's contribution for the needed results. Your coaching can help. Ensure that the manager does not save feedback until it is time for the review, for example—a common bad practice. Positive *and* negative feedback should be given as soon as possible.

More coaching. Give the new manager several assignments with the objective of learning about the peripheries of the job, how it interfaces with other parts of the enterprise, and beyond. Just meeting the key people involved will be beneficial and important for future development. Keep the assignments small in scope—the manager already has one or two other things to do—and explain the reasons for them. They will be accepted enthusiastically, or you chose the wrong manager.

In addition to basic management education and training (perhaps ten days in the first year, dropping to five, thereafter) there will be professional education. You must not only plan and schedule it, you must ensure that time is allocated and that the programme is followed. In today's enterprises, an inadequately prepared manager is like a loose cannon; a danger to everyone, including the manager.

Disposal of the management resource

Your first thoughts may be of the situation in which you have to say that a manager is not suitable or not wanted as a manager any longer. Nobody likes this situation. Some actively avoid it, letting the situation deteriorate. But a manager who has to go is just one of the many varieties of disposal of the management resource (maybe the most unpleasant one). Most of the other situations are more positive.

By 'disposal', we mean an individual leaves a management position within your domain, as a manager. That is to say, the *resource* is gone. The *individual* may still remain if the manager reverts to a non-managerial role within your domain, or the individual may not be present physically any more. Either way, a hole is left behind. Your management resource has been depleted. Part of your job is to manage the disposal processes effectively.

The recurring themes in most of the situations that we discuss below have to do with:

- detecting weak signals and understanding them
- eliminating the vacancy
- impact on the rest of the enterprise
- the fate of the manager disposed of.

We begin with the most negative and dramatic situation and work our way towards the more positive.

Sudden death

These things happen—an accident, a heart attack, a plane crash. In such cases you can do nothing about the manager's fate, but there may be a family, overwhelmed by grief. They need support, regarding insurance, pension and other financial matters, and even more mundane things like what to do with the company car. Your Personnel function will be better equipped than you to give such support, and they should know all the policy aspects. So, establish contact with them as soon as possible and check from time to time that things are happening properly. Then, devote your time and energy to your own domain and people. They need you.

The manager's colleagues—and you—have been reminded that nobody is immortal. Perhaps they have started to think about their own values in life, the balance between work and private and family life, and whether something ought to change. You are not meant to be a therapist, but you must be very observant and watch how each individual reacts. You should be prepared to be a sounding board and spend time on these sorts of questions.

The people in the late manager's group will have similar feelings. At the very least, they will feel somewhat insecure, as they would with any other unexpected change. An established relationship no longer exists. The new manager is not yet appointed. When you struggle to find a replacement, whether permanent or temporary, you must consider these particular feelings of the group and not just how to get the wheels turning again.

You have to recover swiftly, and with the least possible turbulence. This really points up your planning and acquisition processes. You are in a much better position if you already have a list of people with management potential, and you know their strengths and weaknesses. Brenda did a good job of this aspect of her management work. Bruno was too busy fighting fires, but at least he now has a personnel-related objective regarding identifying potential management candidates.

There is often a delay before the new manager is on board, and you may have to find a temporary solution. You have several options: a deputy from within the group, one of your other managers, or yourself. However, we stress that the person chosen must have the time and the capability to take care of the human side, too, and not just the operation.

Long illness

Here, you really *can* do something in the disposal processes. The objective must be to monitor the situation so that the affected manager can have a dignified departure, without prejudicing the running of the manager's group.

There comes a point where the individual can no longer perform any job of value to the enterprise. Early retirement is the solution. For the manager concerned, the road to insight and acceptance may be very painful, however. You must take a firm stand. At the same time, offer all kinds of support that may be available (talk to your colleagues in Personnel) to make the transition easier. Maybe you can use the experience of someone else who has had to manage this kind of situation.

Sometimes the individual wants to stick to the management job. Indeed, it may be the best possible therapy for this person. It seems to be the easy solution, but is it? Any management job today that is worthy of the name is very demanding. It is out of the question that a person with these severe limitations can fill it—remember, we are discussing people who are ill and deteriorating, *not* physically handicapped managers. While it would certainly show great respect to the individual to preserve the status quo, it would not be respectful to let the manager's subordinates and the rest of the enterprise suffer.

Firing a manager

Fire, terminate, sack, separate—choose your own euphemism. This manager simply has to go! Let us first discuss why. Some instances are obvious. Others are not so clear cut. Criminal behaviour, such as embezzlement or theft belong in the obvious category. What about cheating with expense accounts or exchanging air tickets for cheaper alternatives, then pocketing the money thus saved? This, too, is theft, and most enterprises do not condone stealing on the part of managers or any other employees. So, the guilty party still has to go. Nevertheless, the prevailing culture in some enterprises lets such things happen. What should your position be if you work in one of these? Our suggestion is that you try to establish a higher ethical level, at least within *your* domain. Criminal or unethical behaviour has been brought to the surface and you, as a middle manager, should not condone it in any way. People may enjoy the 'benefits' of lax management, but at the expense of their opinion of the enterprise. Working to high ethical standards brings pride to other aspects of work, too. Your managers must be seen to be setting the example. You have to agree standards with them, and what changes need to be made.

The above cases can generally be supported by hard facts and proved. Remember the Martin case? David accused him of being incompetent as a manager. It was not obvious to you, in the beginning, whether this was true or not. This uncertainty often exists in cases like drug abuse, disloyalty towards the enterprise, displaying religious or racial prejudices, sexual harassment and so on. Disciplinary actions are relatively rare. It is possible that you are not experienced or up to date on the procedural guidelines to follow. Our advice is always to consult the best available expertise on employment rights and legislation, starting in your own enterprise. A mistake here can be very costly for your enterprise and for you.

Often, the peers of this manager and people in the manager's group know what is going on before you do. So, when the situation becomes clear to you, swift action is required to maintain morale within the rest of your domain. Consider using incidents like these for discussions with your managers and within their groups to restate the values of the enterprise and their interpretation in real life.

The failed manager

According to the textbook, this is an easy case. The manager's objectives and goals are agreed and, when they are consistently not met, the manager must be replaced. It was never this easy in practice and in today's turbulent world, new difficulties are added. In all enterprises, employees are able to identify poor managers. Then they wonder why top management does not seem to care about it. Many of the inadequate managers are completely unaware of their inadequacy. They get no feedback on their management capability. In fact, they are often praised by their manager. Middle managers look the other way, hoping that the problem will disappear. Such miracles are as yet unknown. All this is far from the textbook description.

How has this happened? Why are you facing this situation, which is so unfortunate for you and for the manager concerned? Probably you (or one of your predecessors) failed in one or more of the processes earlier in the chain. You appointed the wrong person for the wrong reasons. You did not introduce the manager properly to the specific tasks of being a manager. You did not support the manager's continued development. You did not think of the unique motivational factors for this individual and show your personal interest. Your motivational tools were pep talks, good performance appraisals and a lot of, 'Well done!', even if it was not. Who is really the inadequate manager? Perhaps you?

If the above description fits, you have an obligation to help this manager find a place where the individual is useful and appreciated. There must have been *some* relevant qualities to start with, when somebody made this person a manager. The qualities of a professional may still be excellent. A preference for professional work may be behind the reasons for failure. This individual will probably not be good as a manager somewhere else. Resist the temptation to 're-package' in order to sell the manager off to some distant part of the enterprise. On the other hand, do not rule out completely the possibility of a management job elsewhere. There may be an opportunity with entirely different requirements, where a fresh start can be made and success can follow. However, the most likely solution is a move to a non-management position. We shall discuss this shortly.

The journey to this conclusion can be very painful, both for the manager and for you, especially if you share responsibility for the situation. The manager may display denial, doubt, confusion, anger, refuse to talk with you and so on, but the facts are clear and cannot be denied. This manager cannot remain, but your commitment to finding a new solution must be equally clear.

The redundant manager

Enterprises down-size and outsource, reducing the number of employees and managers. People have to go, in spite of being perfectly capable in their jobs. Perhaps you sigh with relief that you are not personally responsible for these strategic decisions—it is all due to forces beyond your control—but you have to *implement* the disposal processes.

It can be a traumatic experience for the affected manager, as one of them told us:

> I just stood up and left the room and walked around town for two hours.
> I was in a state of shock. Today, three years later, I realize that it was
> the happiest day of my life! Instead of remaining in a job where I had
> already stayed too long, I got a new job which is much more
> challenging and rewarding.

This kind of happy outcome is not unusual, but it does not make the message—'you have to go'—any easier to accept. Managers are often older and they may have left their professional expertise behind. They have more to lose, and finding a new job is difficult enough without the doubtful merit of having been made redundant. When breaking the news, you have to make it crystal clear that the manager has to go. Otherwise, the manager will leave the room and still believe that everything is all right. The first talk is possibly not the time to talk in detail about future alternatives and the support the manager will get. Set up another meeting to discuss this. You have to concentrate on the basic message: the manager has to leave the job and the enterprise.

During your next meeting (which should be held very soon afterwards) you will have to answer the question why the enterprise, which the manager has served so loyally and unselfishly for so many years, suddenly ignores all this and treats the manager this way. It is essential that you know any relevant facts and figures that may explain why this action is necessary. It does not help the affected manager very much, but it is the only correct answer. Maybe the revenues and funds available do not allow the enterprise to operate at the same level as before. A surgical operation is necessary or the body is going to die. This is also the time to start talking about the new future, the support programme you can offer and to introduce the outplacement consultant service, if this is part of the programme.

An outplacement service is expensive, but it gives positive benefits both to the enterprise and to the manager. Many outplacement consultants offer a room within their own premises where the affected managers can conduct job-hunting activities. There is a place to go each morning where there is support, both from the staff and from others in the same situation. The enterprise avoids the potentially awkward situation of having a dissatisfied individual mingle with the staff who have not been affected.

Another lesson to draw from this is the necessity for managers to maintain their professional or industry knowledge, in short, to maintain their external market value. As a middle manager, you have an important role to convince them that this is necessary, and to support such activities.

We have already discussed Brenda. She wanted a change, but wanted to stay within the enterprise. What, though, of the manager who leaves for an attractive offer from outside? Once again, you should find out what lies behind the decision. Perhaps it is for a job with less pay and, perhaps, less status. In this case, you have some serious questions to answer. Your boss will ask them, anyway. Your other managers and their people may know the answers.

Have you neglected this individual's drive and capability to move on to greater responsibilities? Have you even been guilty of blocking possible promotions (or sideways moves) because the manager was 'indispensable' in the present job? Well, from now on, you will *have* to do without this manager.

Is the offered job one for which this manager would never have qualified in your enterprise? Say farewell, with your best wishes. This is a chance the individual must take.

The regressive manager

Brenda wanted to remain in the enterprise, maybe even in your domain, but not as a manager. Your approach was to try to retain her as a manager, somewhere in the enterprise, to make use of her qualities and experience, and to avoid sending signals that management jobs are not attractive or desirable. These are valid points. But consider Peter, a former colleague of ours.

Peter was promoted to the post of Field Systems Engineering Manager in a branch sales office. He was the perfect example of the technically brilliant professional. As a systems engineer, he was admired by colleagues and customers alike. Also, he had a friendly, open personality, with a sense of humour to match. However, he was persuaded to take this first-line management job. Now, instead of solving complicated and challenging technical problems and interfacing with customers he had known for years, he saw himself as a mother hen figure to half a dozen former colleagues. After a year or so, he pleaded to be given his old job back. He got it, and he never moved from that branch office. Geographically, it was where he wanted to be. He retired a happy, plateaued man, still admired and respected by all.

The last few words of the above are important. If a manager wants to go back to a professional job, how do you ensure a dignified departure? In many cases, going back means loss of status and prestige, but this was *not* the case with Peter. This can really get in the way of implementing the move, and it is a move that really ought to be made. You must demonstrate (at all times, not just on this occasion) that professional and management jobs are equally important in terms of contribution. They are different, that is all. You also have to support the individual fully, particularly with any necessary education and other developmental activities needed to fill the new position. The signals you send this way to the rest of the enterprise are as important as the fair treatment of this former manager.

However, do not design special jobs for former managers. Every job must be justified by the needs of the enterprise. We know of many cases where former managers have been moved into support roles with a new job title that includes the word 'manager'. Then, because they have considerable experience, they quickly grasped the exclusive right to information, decisions or recommendations. This is not normally in the best interest of the enterprise. The former manager must understand the new role and that the new power base is very different now.

Retirement

Unlike early retirement, which we have discussed earlier in relation to prolonged illness or down-sizing, normal retirement should present you with no surprises. You know about it years beforehand. You have plenty of time to exercise your acquisition processes to find and prepare the replacement manager (if needed) and plan an elegant departure for the retiring manager. There should be no problem here.

However, some individuals do not want to retire. Their work gives them value and self-esteem and they feel that they still have a lot more to contribute. They may well be right. However, apart from exceptional cases, you should stick to the planned date. This may be one of the rare promotion opportunities for your key people. The new manager can bring a fresh approach, try new methods, establish new relations. This is rarely the case with a manager on the threshold of normal retirement age. However, the retired manager who still wants to contribute could use skills and energy in other ways, by involvement in local government, charity organizations, sport and so on. You can plant these ideas and even help with contacts and introductions. It is no bad thing for the image of your enterprise to have its loyal and skilled former managers involved in such activities.

Indeed, you should ask yourself whether or not this individual really should remain a manager until the last working day. In the last few years or months, will new ventures or daring decisions be taken for some unknown person to have the satisfaction of implementing? Perhaps worse, grand decisions may be taken in the hope that the manager's name will go down in history, but without having to take full responsibility and accountability for all the hard and risky work involved. It may be better to use this experienced manager as an internal consultant, a leader of special task forces or as a mentor for younger managers at the end of the manager's career.

Promotion

The best form of disposal is when the manager is so good that someone else in the enterprise is clamouring for their needed talents and skills. 'Needed' is the key word. It means you have done such a good job of the planning, acquisition and stewardship processes that the manager is recognized as being ready to make a bigger contribution than at present. The recognition may be yours alone, of course. You may wish to promote the manager concerned within your domain, or the need may be beyond your domain, a promotion to some other part of the enterprise.

This manager is a 'star'. You are very happy to have such a manager and you would like to keep this individual for ever, but this is just wishful thinking. Other people will quickly recognize the manager's abilities. Offers will be made, sometimes subtle, sometimes not. So, the potential and value soon become clear to the manager concerned. We suggest you take a realistic approach and actively coach this individual for greater responsibilities. By doing so, you will also be able to discuss any shortcomings and needs for development, and prevent a premature move. You must provide visibility to top management and other key people. Much of this may be against your natural instincts, but you really have no choice. If you do not plan the disposal of this manager, you will be taken by surprise one day.

Another thing. The manager concerned will spread the word that you are an excellent middle manager. You take good care of your managers and you deserve their best efforts in return. The best managers will want to work for you, so you still come out smelling like roses, and you have gained at least one more important ally in your personal network. We shall be discussing this in more detail in Part 6, 'Maintaining your own development'.

Until now, we have concentrated on what we see as the basic, even mundane tasks and responsibilities of any middle manager; the tools of the trade. However, our aim is not to perpetuate and preserve traditional roles and behaviour, to pass on to you and for you to pass on to your successors. Rather, we hope you are now well enough equipped to maximize the Total Quality of your management resource. This includes the management resource that is embodied within *you*.

We have emphasized that traditional organization structures are being replaced by new ones, Still, you may feel that we have used many traditional references. This is true. To understand our rationale, consider Figure P5.1.

Our main focus has been on excellent quality of management, and we believe that the principles discussed here are appropriate to any organization structure, but the difficulties are largest during the periods of transition.

Härje Franzén led a management benchmarking study in five major Swedish international enterprises. All of them, despite solid, good reputations for management and personnel practices, barely reached the borderline between poor and excellent management. We believe that most enterprises today are positioned in the lower left-hand quadrant of Figure P5.1, that is, most enterprises have substantially less than excellent management quality and they have a traditional, hierarchic organization structure.

Nevertheless, we believe that a move to the top right-hand quadrant is, or will be,

SOFTLY, SOFTLY VERSUS BIG BANG

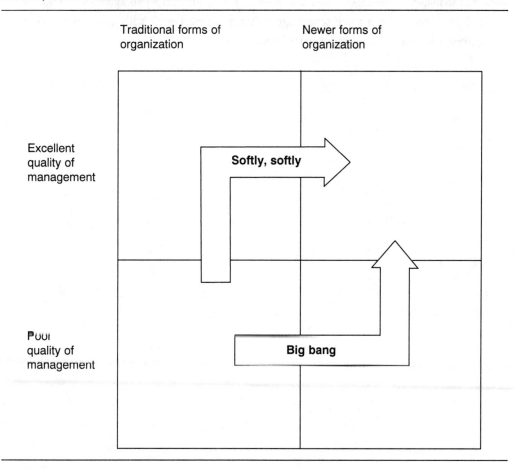

Figure P5.1

necessary for reasons of cost or competitiveness. There are two strategies for moving from the bottom left to the top right. One strategy is to change the organization (the big bang option), hoping that the problems will go away and that a new and appropriate quality of management will appear, somehow. This might be exciting, but we suggest that it is a vain hope. The other strategy is to realize the considerable improvements that can be made within the prevailing structure. We hope you have noticed that the excellent quality of management that results will benefit the enterprise even if structural changes do not occur. More important, however, is that such an excellent quality of management will lubricate the difficulties of transition from one structure to the other. This is a simplified description, but we believe that the second approach (the softly, softly option) is the best. You are moving towards your goal from the starting point and through familiar territory, instead of navigating in the white areas of the map—where lurk the dragons and monsters.

In Part 6, we turn to your own continued development. You have to be more than an excellent manager of managers. You also have to play your part as an agent of change for the good of your enterprise, a more senior agent than your managers, with more resources, more clout, armed with a broader and deeper knowledge.

■ PART 6

MAINTAINING YOUR OWN DEVELOPMENT

Your job—manager or leader?

Let us nail this question straight away. As a middle manager, you have to be both a manager *and* a leader. You have probably already exhibited some leadership qualities. Hopefully, they were a factor leading to your promotion or hiring to a middle management position. However, now, particularly as a middle manager in the changing organizational structures we discussed earlier, your leadership qualities will have to be outstanding.

Don't believe that excellent leaders are born that way. There are basic skills to be developed, and knowledge to be acquired for a leader, just as for a manager—it isn't all charisma and seat-of-the-pants. Some people can never become good managers. Equally, some people can never become good leaders. Therefore, some managers can never become good leaders. The latter group might include the good managers who really are good *administrators*— excellent at keeping the wheels turning smoothly and preserving the status quo.

Good leaders not only thrive on coping with change, they *need* it. The best of them do not wait for things to happen, they have such good sources and flows of information, and such good forecasting techniques, that they *anticipate* change. Then, they exploit the opportunities inherent in the change. They *proactively* exploit these opportunities rather than passively react to the change when it hits them. Even better, excellent leaders *make change happen*. They challenge the status quo and force change into the enterprise. They are not averse to risk, but they know where they are going.

Naturally, they cannot do it alone. A leader alone is not a leader. Look over your shoulder from time to time. If your people are following you (rather than being dragged along in your wake), you are a leader. Leaders have followers, enthusiastic followers.

You must have met, seen or even worked for someone who had excellent leadership qualities. What are these qualities? Think about it for a few minutes, then write them down. Our list follows.

Qualities of leadership

Ours is not an exhaustive list (as usual, please add any that you may have considered important and are missing from our list), but it includes the main ones, which are:

- the ability to inspire and motivate others
- can create excitement in others
- can create pride in others
- can align different people and groups—creating effective coalitions
- visible competence and credibility—people believe their message

- decent behaviour, modesty, patience, sensitivity, politeness, trust and so on
- well informed
- clear vision—'this is where we are going'
- loyalty to followers
- prepared to take risks, but consistently delivers results
- not afraid of strength in associates or subordinates.

Notice that almost all of these characteristics are to do with behaviour and attitude rather than expertise or cleverness; wisdom as much as intellect. Expertise is relatively easy to buy or hire. Leadership has never been in such short supply, or in such demand, at all levels. It is essential for you to develop your leadership qualities, not only for your present job, but to demonstrate your fitness for future promotion. Also, by example and other means, you must develop the leadership qualities of your managers.

> *Business Week* carried an article in the issue of 23 August 1993 that looked at the growing numbers of CEOs of large companies—IBM and Kodak, for example—who have been moved on to be replaced by outsiders. It is happening in many smaller companies, too. The headhunting agencies searching for their replacements, people who will shake up the established way of doing things, if necessary, are looking for leaders rather than managers. When search consultant (that is, headhunter) E. Pendleton James was asked to find a new CEO for an insurance company, he asked the client to identify the attributes it was seeking. 'Leadership', came the reply over the Boardroom table. 'I'm not too concerned if the CEO knows much about the industry.'

Our list shows some of the important qualities of leadership. How can you develop them in yourself?

First, there are the behavioural aspects. With 'decent behaviour', we mentioned modesty, patience, sensitivity, politeness. We are not aware of any management development programmes, books or videos that will make you more modest, more patient, more sensitive or more polite. You have to look to yourself, and the responses of those around you, to develop these attributes. There is also the small word, 'trust' on this list. This means that your followers trust *you*. We *can* help you to do something about building the climate of trust that is so essential for effective leadership. That is why there is a special section of the topic in this book (see 'The climate of trust', pages 71–76).

However, it takes time and effort to build a climate of trust, and it can be destroyed so easily and quickly, particularly by ignoring the other behavioural attributes of politeness, sensitivity and so forth. Beware of betraying a confidence, breaking a promise, humiliating one of your managers or one of their people in public, lying, using scorn, sarcasm or derision, being disdainful of other people's efforts and so on.

These behavioural aspects, the example that you set, are *necessary* for effective leadership. In fact, your attitude to subordinates is possibly the most important factor of all. It is not *sufficient*, however. You also have to be able to inspire others to follow you into the world of risk, change and yet more change. It has to look like it is worth doing, to have a feeling of excitement, of reward and pride in having participated. This is where you not only have to communicate your vision (or whatever you want to call it) well and sensitively, it has to be the *right* vision—a winner.

Getting the right vision

Be aware of the fine distinction between vision, in the sense of discernment or foresight, and some of its synonyms, like hallucination, a delusion. By vision, we mean a business-orientated definition of the desired future. Vision has to do with seeing and pictures. Close your eyes and the vision should be there. It should not contain tables of numbers and abstract descriptions. An example is John F. Kennedy's, 'Put a man on the moon before 1970, and bring him back alive'.

Excellent leaders not only have the *right* vision, *they have the capacity to transform the vision into reality and elicit commitment to it from others.* They *involve* their followers in developing scenarios for the future.

After you have created and agreed your vision for your domain, involve all your managers. Present it to your management committee. Ask your managers to suggest, for example, what might happen between now and, say, two years' time (choose your own timeframe) that would dramatically impact the required results from your total domain. Just brainstorm them. The impacts could range from very positive to very negative. Possible areas to consider might include:

- your industry
- competition
- technology
- economic developments
- exchange rates
- political changes
- internal structure
- international developments
- social changes
- new skills/competencies and so forth.

Ask your managers to reflect on the list they have created. If you have, say, six managers, discuss and decide at your next meeting which six factors are most likely, and what would be the impact if they should happen. Give one to each manager, with responsibility to monitor, study, analyse and report back to the management committee, regularly. The amount of shared knowledge of potentially critical issues will be impressive. So will the learning, the feeling of collective participation in things that are critically important (*they* decided what should be on the list, after all), but are probably outside the scope of your managers' day-to-day work. You will be ready, as a team, to anticipate or react effectively, to exploit the opportunity or to crush the problem.

Delegation

Excellent leaders delegate. Trust downwards generates trust upwards. You have to translate the vision into projects that will have tangible results (such as the IBM laptop PC we described earlier), with milestones and completion dates. Then you must delegate responsibility for these projects to your managers. Let them (and their people) determine *how* to do it and make it happen in practice.

Your bureaucratic power to command and control as a middle manager is already substantially less than it was a decade ago, so delegation is not only a good thing, you really have not got much option. This makes the *need* for excellent leadership much more important today. Your managers and their people will be working a lot of the time out of your sight, and often out of sight of each other. They will be in cross-functional or cross-company teams, maybe working will alliance partners or customers or suppliers, often with people (as project or team colleagues) who are *senior to you* in their own organizations. Your people are 'empowered' whether you like it or not. However, the thing that binds them to you and your enterprise, its values and policies, and the need to deliver the needed results is your leadership qualities. The fact that you are the boss will become less and less important.

Excellent leaders *involve* their followers in developing scenarios for the future. Your monthly review meetings and your management committee should be excellent for this, as well as for the more formal aspects of monitoring and communicating.

Finally, excellent leaders are good at focusing their own time and energy. Delegation is only part of the means of doing this. They also know precisely which are the limited number of matters on which to devote their special talents, the matters that will have the biggest long-term impact on the enterprise.

Preparing for your future

The agent of change

Now that you have a grip on the Total Quality of your managers, think about yourself for a change. We shall assume that by using the tools and techniques we have discussed up to now. and by managing *through* your managers, your domain is efficient, effective and that the level of employee (and manager) satisfaction is high. Let us turn to your other major responsibility: the agent of change.

Given your more senior position and perspective, and larger resources, you have to look for and exploit bigger paradigm shifts; the bigger payoff opportunities. You have to envisage innovation that is far beyond the apparent scope of your job. You cannot do it alone. You have neither the necessary power nor the resources. Just as you 'operate' your domain through your managers, you have to accomplish the larger, innovative achievements *through other people*—colleagues, customers, suppliers, alliance partners and so on. You have to go out and secure the additional strength and resources to make these things happen, the entrepreneurial new initiatives.

First, how do you identify the innovative opportunities? You look, you listen, you ask, you 'think crazy', you constantly challenge the status quo. Ask yourself, frequently, 'If we were to start all over again tomorrow, would we do this thing this way? Would we do it at all?' It is not easy; it requires constant practise.

Try to imagine being a banker 25 years ago. This was how customers withdrew cash from the bank. They stood in a queue, for quite some time, during the few hours that the bank was open to the public (it was even worse at lunchtimes). A clerk scrutinized the cheque or withdrawal slip, scrutinized the customer, scrutinized the customer's records, counted the money and handed it over. There was a strong focus on having a skilled individual between the customer and where the money was kept. It had been like this for 200 years or so.

Then, someone comes along with the crazy idea of knocking a big hole in the wall of the bank and installing a machine full of the bank's money. It coughs out the money when a piece of plastic is shoved into it and four digits are entered. It does it, unattended, 24 hours a day, 7 days a week. Top managers, typically, do not get ridiculous ideas like this (or like giving purchase order entry terminals to customers, for example), but *someone* had to challenged the established way of doing things, even though it was totally against the banking culture of the time.

This 'somebody', typically, is a middle manager or someone within a middle manager's domain. Either way, *you* have to get it done.

This is more a question of attitudes than knowledge or skill. Test your own attitudes on the next case.

> Assume you work for a company selling products and services to other enterprises. You will not thrive unless customer satisfaction is high. You have various schemes to encourage your people to work towards all aspects of customer satisfaction.
>
> Then, somebody comes up with an idea. It is to replace all current customer satisfaction programmes with a letter to be sent to all key customers, once per year. It says, 'Dear Customer. As you know, our objective is that you will be delighted with our products, services and all other aspects of doing business with us. We want all our people to do their utmost to sustain this goal. Please take the enclosed cheque for £500 and give it to the individual in our company who has given you excellent service, with our thanks attached. Should you decide that none of our people merits this award, please keep the cheque, or give it to a charity of your choice, and accept our apology and our promise to improve'.

Notice that this places the decision where it belongs—with the customer (see the definition of Total Quality on page 44). It also gives an opportunity, once a year, to underline your dedication to all aspects of customer satisfaction.

Over to you

So, what is your immediate reaction to this idea? Please write it down now.

Here are some reactions from real managers to whom this idea was put:

Good idea in theory. But we can't trust our customers. They will just keep the money, and push us all the harder.

Interesting suggestion. Can you tell me of any other company that has used this successfully?

Nice idea. But it won't work because ... [list of objections]

Thank you. We really need ideas like this. I'll think about it. (Then there is silence.)

These answers tell you something about people's attitudes to innovation. You will certainly come across many more, including some of the following old chestnuts, but watch out for such words coming readily from *your* lips.

- 'We tried that before.'
- 'It costs too much.'
- 'That's not my job.'
- 'We don't have the time.'
- 'Our organization is too small.'
- 'We've never done it before.'
- 'It runs up our overhead.'
- 'That's not our problem.'
- 'Why? It's still working OK.'
- 'We're not ready for that.'
- 'We don't have the personnel.'

- 'Good thought, but impractical.'

- 'Our place is different'
- 'That's beyond our responsibility.'
- 'It's too radical a change.'
- 'Not enough resources.'
- 'We're all too busy to do that.'
- 'It's against policy.'
- 'We don't have the authority.'
- 'Too blue sky. Let's get back to reality.'
- 'You're right, but .'
- 'You're two years ahead of your time.'
- 'We don't have the equipment/room/and so on.'

- 'Can't teach an old dog new tricks.'

Your future development will not take place in a stable world because such a world does no exist. Your best option is to change the world around you, and develop with it.

Your network

Excellent leaders keep on winning not only because of personal leadership qualities. They are also supported by excellent information networks. They develop, cultivate, maintain and keep open a network of contacts all over the place. Above all else, excellent leaders are well-informed. No matter how high you rise in the enterprise, keep your information channels open—all of them. Without them, you will be fed with whatever your subordinates decide you should get. The more levels there are in the hierarchy, the more waste bins and information filters there are, and this filtering can be highly selective.

This information network does not necessarily mean having a powerful desktop computer, connected to all kinds of electronic highways and databases, though you need this too, in the 1990s. Rather, it means having extensive, informal networks within and beyond the enterprise. These are so important that, if yours do not properly exist yet, creating them must be of high priority to sustain your leadership role. This is particularly so for a middle manager appointed from outside the enterprise or from some remote division, so far as the *internal* network is concerned. Work at it hard and fast if this describes you.

However, your network is not only the means to acquire information of all kinds. It is also a critically important vehicle for you *to get things done*. It is the means to enable you to get access to power and resources, far beyond those that came with your job description. The more networks in which you are involved, and the more extensive they are, the better. They are much more effective as 'enablers' than any power that you may believe you have by virtue of your elevated position in the hierarchy. With excellent networks, you can identify which group of managers has the right combination of business skills, needs, judgement, personal motivation, power and control of resources to act as champions for your innovative idea. This inevitably means that you must think and act cross-functionally. Many other domains will have a stake in your projects.

> The bank cash dispensing machines illustrate the importance of this. Chemical Bank was the first to install such machines in New York, in 1969. The goal was simply to automate the clerk's job. The focus was on reducing costs; a very localized, departmental view. It did not work, so Chemical Bank withdrew the machines.
>
> In contrast, someone in Citicorp saw automatic cash dispensers as being a powerful marketing tool—a totally different viewpoint. The bank did a lot of research on customer attitudes and responses. Much friendlier machines were built. By covering New York City with them in the late 1970s, Citicorp more than doubled its current and deposit accounts and increased market share from 5 to 13 per cent.

This was far more than an automation exercise. Many other functions in the bank (and its customers) were involved in making it work well and in benefiting from its success. *Somebody* had to identify them as potential stakeholders, explain, negotiate, sell, persuade and all the rest.

Your network has to include your manager and all the top management team. You have to know which people at the top have the power to influence your innovative projects; who will be for, who will be against. Even for projects that originate within you and can be supported entirely *by* you, this is still important. Even a general expression of support from the top can make it a lot easier to sell the project to your own people, as well as to others.

The ability to secure critical resources is one of the quality measurements we suggested earlier. Your network is truly a critical resource. Who should be in it? How can you go about expanding it, lubricating the lines of communication?

CHECK-LIST 18   Your network

Who?

☐ your managers and their people

☐ your peers

☐ your manager

☐ top management

☐ customers—internal and external

☐ suppliers—internal and external

☐ alliance partners

☐ trade and industry associations

☐ relevant government agencies

☐ key opinion formers and so forth (you should be able to add plenty of items to this list to make it specific to your own situation).

Your extended network:

☐ trade and industry journals

☐ abstracting services

☐ media, such as *The Economist, Business Week,* the *Financial Times*

☐ consumer surveys

☐ market research surveys and so forth.

We suggest you start by adding names of real people, real trade journals and so forth to th check-list above. What patterns do you see? Is your network concentrated in just one or two categories? Should you not broaden its scope, include new kinds of relationships?

Another useful exercise is to tick off the people you can turn to and who will support you when there is a critical issue and you need help. Even an impressively large network can shrink dramatically when you look at it this way. Is its shrunken size a reflection of *your* previous lack of support for others?

Building your network

Use your monthly review meetings. Beware of the Persian Messenger Syndrome; you should be *rewarding* the first person who brings you the bad news! It is vital that subordinates are comfortable about delivering unpleasant messages to you. We are back again to the climate of trust.

One of your responsibilities is to stifle serious problems before they blow up and damage the enterprise. The sooner the problem is revealed, diagnosed and corrected, the better. If you find you are receiving only good news, you can be sure that you are not seeing the complete picture.

Use your management committee. Invite key internal suppliers and customers, fellow middle managers, perhaps. Ask them to present what they do and how your domain affects theirs. Invite key *external* suppliers and customers as well, and ask them to do the same thing, *then keep the lines of communication open and well used.* Similarly, invite members of the top management team, who plan to be in the vicinity, particularly if they are from an area of the enterprise that is geographically or functionally remote from yours.

Search for any signs of turbulence in the enterprise. Find out where new things are being tried out, innovation in technology, procedures, *anything*, then get yourself involved, even if it has no apparent bearing on what you are doing today. Force yourself into it, somehow. Beware of the steady state. It may be peaceful, but there is not much for you to learn there.

Visit external customers, if you have any. If any of the business processes in your domain are customer-visible, then you have external customers. How often do you think that the owner of the process 'bill customers' ever visits the customers of this process? We mean the *real* customers, the people who are the users of it, or the victims of its bad performance? Not often. Yet, how much could be learned! What percentage of your time do you spend in front of external customers? How can you possibly know what are their real (and changing) needs? This means real opportunities for the enterprise or early avoidance of problems. Too many people in your position keep themselves too remote from external customers. Again, we are not talking about the pleasant visits to senior managers of your customers. Rather, we are talking about the people who depend on the quality of your customer-visible processes. Equally, you should visit *internal* customers, of course, to keep open the lines of communication *and to learn.*

Visit internal and external suppliers and strategic alliance partners, too. Particularly in today's more widely extended enterprises, they are key components of your network.

Find out which trade or industry associations are involved with your enterprise, national and international standards organizations, government bodies, and so on. Get yourself nominated as a representative of your enterprise.

Watch out for conferences, seminars, workshops and so forth that relate to your enterprise. Attend as a participant, even as a speaker, if possible. Extend your network and keep these lines of communication open.

We cannot overemphasize the importance of your network. It does not come with the job. You have to build it yourself. But it addresses two critical needs. One is the need to gain access to information, resources and support. The second is the need to get cooperation to do whatever is necessary. This means that you have to develop your political skills. You have to be an excellent negotiator (find a good course, then attend it—soon), a diplomat, a politician, a dealmaker. You cannot justify your salary merely by presiding over your domain. Those days are over. People who make decisions, *then make things happen* are the only middle managers now in demand.

Use the top management members of your network to secure support, sponsorship, resources and so on, but don't go to them, or to your manager, as a means of resolving conflicts with your peers. This so-called escalation procedure might have been appropriate under the old regimes (though we doubt it). Today, you have to accept responsibility for your own actions, even when they impact other parts of the business and beyond. Whenever you go to top management to resolve an issue, you are asking people to stick their necks out, and people at that level are not normally famous for sticking their necks out. Sort it out yourself.

You might start by telling *your* managers that issues escalated to you must be impossible for them to solve. If they bring you problems that are merely concerns, by all means offer to be a discussion partner. If they ask you to do their job, make it clear that it will have an immediate impact on their merit ratings, and it will not be a positive one.

Communication skills

Your role as a communicator is vital, yet many people in your position are absolutely terrible at the basic communication skills. You can do something about it. There are lots of courses to choose from. Have the humility to accept that your communication skills are less than excellent and get yourself on a course.

You will not only have to represent your enterprise to your managers, increasingly you will have to represent it to the outside world. You will become involved in situations with local government bodies, chambers of commerce, in cooperation projects, strategic alliances hosting visitors and so forth.

Some of these tasks can be delegated—indeed they *should* be delegated as part of th development of your managers—but you will become directly involved much more frequently than in the past. You may be involved in radio or television interviews. These, particularly television, are very powerful opportunities to do a really awful job of representing your enterprise. Done well, though, they can give you and your enterprise the best possible form of visibility. Anticipate it. There are courses that teach the basic skills in handling radio and television interviews effectively. Enrol yourself on one, then let it be known. You might then find that you are the natural first choice when the need arises to have someone represent your enterprise in a skilled and articulate manner.

Your role as deputy

You will certainly have to act as deputy for your boss now and then—as a result of sickness, holidays and so forth or maybe permanently in some committees or work groups. These are excellent opportunities to enhance your network. They also provide visibility for you. Ensure that you are well prepared. Find out, for example:

- to what extent you are expected to state the enterprise's position and give commitments
- what your mandate is (make sure it is not too constricting!)
- what additional information and/or education are needed for each of these roles.

The generalist

The effective middle managers in today's enterprises—those who survive—will find that their roles have been expanded and their functions changed. Indeed, at *all* levels, the flattening of organizational structures, the new ways of organizing work and the proliferation of information support systems are placing different demands on people. Formerly, someone might enter a manufacturing plant as an apprentice storekeeper, move on to be a storeman, assistant storekeeper, chief storekeeper or whatever. The individual might have broken out from the stores to become a production control assistant, then proceeded through the plant management hierarchy to become production controller. At each stage, the individual tended to learn only what was required to perform the necessary tasks. Often this knowledge was left behind when moved up to the next rung. Somebody else was doing it. The same thing applied to almost any industry.

Now, the number of layers is smaller, so there is a much *deeper* level of knowledge needed to perform effectively on whatever rung you may happen to be. At the same time, the *horizontal* scope of the work has expanded. Wherever you are, you need to know more about what is happening in adjacent and distant parts of the enterprise and beyond. Information technology not only supports this kind of working, *it empowers the individuals concerned.*

Figure P6.1 shows the way things used to be. People at the top tended to be paid for exercising a large amount of judgement. In taking decisions, they used summarized information from within the enterprise, often quite old information. They relied heavily on information from outside the enterprise—economic and industry trends, competitive information, market trends, exchange rate movements and other financial indicators and so forth.

Nearer the bottom, an apprentice storekeeper (or equivalent) was able to exercise very little judgement. The information needed to do the job effectively was detailed, accurate, up-to-date and voluminous, and nearly all of it originated from within the enterprise. At the bottom, we have robotics where no judgement is exercised but where there are very detailed internal information requirements. Figure P6.1 shows how things changed as you moved up the hierarchy.

HOW THINGS USED TO BE

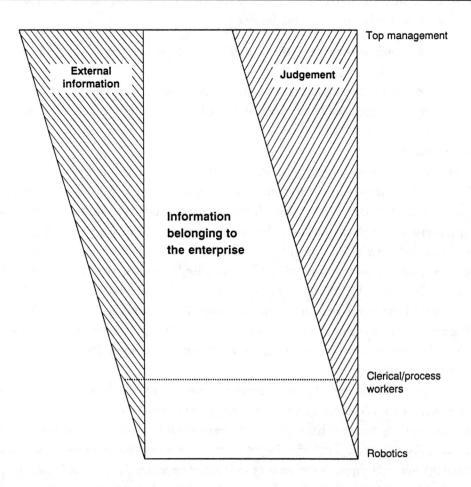

Figure P6.1

Things are different today. Even a relatively new employee in Ford's goods receiving section of the stores is on-line to suppliers, to the procurement and to accounts payable people, and has access to production schedules. The same trend is taking place in other industries.

This need for people with a wider and deeper knowledge applies particularly to middle managers. Top managers do not know how to have their strategies translated into actions to produce results. They delegate it to you. Generalists are needed, not specialists, as enterprises demand solutions to interdisciplinary problems and the exploitation of more holistic opportunities. Nevertheless, it is important that you maintain your professional skills. In the United Kingdom, the Institute of Chartered Accountants runs a wide range of programmes for its members, including some aimed at senior managers, such as chief accountants and finance directors. The idea is to keep them up to date with what is happening in the profession—they may have qualified 10 or 20 years ago. Similar programmes exist for other disciplines, so don't allow yourself to fall behind, and it is another opportunity to extend your network.

However, you really must pay attention to broadening your interests, horizons and knowledge. The skills to analyse, synthesize and conceptualize are much enhanced, and produce a richer result, if you are a person of wide-ranging interests and curiosity. The more things you know about, the more things amaze and fascinate you, the more you will see opportunities to tie together apparently unrelated proposals. This may include coupling to other parts, inside and beyond your domain and your enterprise. It does not require you to be intellectually brilliant, just interested and open to wonder.

If you come from a non-financial background, then (quickly) get some formal education regarding accounts. CEOs may come from a very wide range of disciplines, but the one thing they have in common is the ability to read a balance sheet. You must acquire basic accounting skills as soon as possible. You will need them very soon.

Most of the courses referred to above are of relatively short duration—a few days, maybe a week. You have to make time available in your diary, then do them. Now and again, it might be worthwhile getting away for a two- or three-week period on a course run for senior managers from a variety of industries. Most business schools offer such programmes. For example, the Manchester Business School has run an ever-evolving programme called the Senior Executive Course for many years now. There, you may find yourself with people running coal mines in India, a pharmaceutical company in Brazil, an orthopaedic surgeon from the United Kingdom's National Health Service, a banker from Cyprus or a marketing manager from a brewery, for example. Three weeks of intensive business school curriculum with a richly varied group of participants like this is a very broadening experience, and your network expands again. Similar programmes to the Manchester Senior Executive Course are available in many other places.

Sometimes, business schools run single-enterprise management and executive development programmes. Here, there is usually the same rich variation of participants, but they all come from the same enterprise. Some enterprises have their own education centres, of course, such as the Civil Service, Safeway, IBM, the major banks and oil companies, for example. They run similar in-house management and executive programmes. In any case, find out what is available and enrol yourself on your chosen course or courses. Again, your personal network as an information source *and as an enabler* will be substantially enhanced. When you can put a face to the voice at the other end of the telephone line, and vice versa, it is much easier to communicate or ask for help.

The excellent middle manager

There is not much formal education that is specifically aimed at middle managers, which is largely the reason for this book. The following is a list of attributes that we believe an excellent middle manager should have. They have all been referred to earlier. We summarize them here so that they can form a framework for discussing your future self-development.

- *has overview and foresight* You know what is going on over a much wider perspective than that of your own domain and you can develop alternative scenarios about what will happen in the future
- *communicates the vision* You engage everyone in your picture of the desired future
- *works through managers* You trust your managers and give them independence and support
- *drives change* Otherwise, you are merely an administrator. But with your overview and foresight, you can see that change is inevitable and you create an environment in which new ideas and suggestions emerge naturally, involving as many people as possible in decisions—they are your change agents
- *focuses own time and energy* If everything is important, then nothing is important
- *solves conflicts* You are sensitive to differences between people, groups and departments, you are patient, you are a good listener and you do not 'shoot from the hip'
- *is a good judge of people* You can help them to exploit their strengths and improve their areas of weakness, but you can live with the ambiguities of imperfection in everyone, including yourself

● *represents the enterprise and senior management* You are not only fully aware of what is going on (you have overview and foresight), you are an important channel for information down from senior management. You not only communicate well, you also have excellent feedback mechanisms to confirm that the message was received and understood the way you wanted it to be
● *is a good role model* You behave to your managers in a manner that is consistent with how you want them to behave with their people.

The tools and check-lists should help you with many of these attributes. Your attitude to learning is even more important. Bear in mind that promotion opportunities are even more limited for you than for the managers reporting to you. This is just simple arithmetic. You should be thinking less about, 'How can I prepare myself for my next promotion?' and more about 'What do I need to learn so that I can decide where to go and what to do next?'

We end with a passage from 'The New Managerial Work' by Rosabeth Moss Kanter, *Harvard Business Review*, November–December, 1989:

> The book is gone. In the new corporation, managers have only themselves to count on for success. They must learn to operate without the crutch of hierarchy. Position, title and authority are no longer adequate tools, not in a world where subordinates are encouraged to think for themselves and where managers have to work synergistically with other departments and even other companies. Success depends increasingly on tapping into sources of good ideas, figuring out whose co-operation is needed to act on those ideas, and working with both to produce results. In short, the new managerial work implies very different ways of obtaining and using power.

The old book may be gone. We hope this new one will help you to acquire and use this power to produce results.

Index

INDEX